FICHTENBERG'S GUIDE
TO MAKING FANCY PAPER

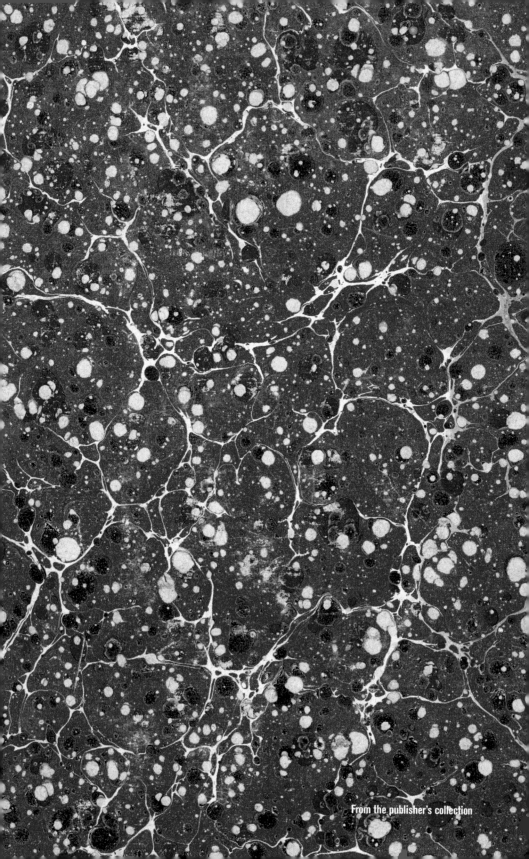

FICHTENBERG'S GUIDE TO MAKING FANCY PAPER

Marbled Paper, Monochromatic *and* Colored Papers, Specialty *and* Metallic Papers, Sealing Wax, etc.

BY

M. FICHTENBERG

OF PARIS

TRANSLATED BY

Debra G. Tremper

2023
SIX PENNY GRAPHICS
FREDERICKSBURG, VIRGINIA

Fichtenberg's Guide to Making Fancy Paper: Marbled Paper, Monochromatic and Colored Papers, Specialty and Metallic Papers, Sealing Wax, Etc. by M. Fichtenberg.
Translated and annotated by Debra G. Tremper

Published by Six Penny Graphics, Fredericksburg, Virginia.

ISBN: 978-1-7326595-6-8

Contents

SUPPLEMENTAL MATERIAL

List of Paper Patterns

Safety

Many of the ingredients and techniques listed in this text are toxic, dangerous, or both.

Proceed with the utmost caution and investigate the safe handling of all materials before using them. Always use appropriate safety equipment and ensure adequate ventilation.

Approximate Conversions from Metric to U.S. Measures[1]

The numerical value of the units in the **When You Know** column is multiplied by the **approximate** unit conversion factor found in the **Multiply By** column to obtain a numerical value for the units listed in the To **Find Column.**

		Length		
Symbol	**When You Know**	**Multiply By**	**To Find**	**Symbol**
mm	millimeter	0.04	inch	in
cm	centimeter	0.39	inch	in
m	meter	3.28	foot	ft

		Mass (weight)		
Symbol	**When You Know**	**Multiply By**	**To Find**	**Symbol**
g	gram	0.04	ounce	oz
kg	kilogram	2.20	pound	lb

		Volume		
Symbol	**When You Know**	**Multiply By**	**To Find**	**Symbol**
L	liter	2.11	pint, liquid	pt
L	liter	1.06	quart, liquid	qt
L	liter	0.26	gallon	gal

		Temperature (exact)		
Symbol	**When You Know**	**Calculation**	**To Find**	**Symbol**
°C	degree Celsius	multiply 1.8, then add 32	degree Fahrenheit	°F

---

1 "Approximate Conversions from Metric to U.S. Customary Measures" NIST Physical Measurement Laboratory: Office of Weights and Measures. https://www.nist.gov/pml/owm/approximate-conversions-metric-us-customary-measures (Retrieved September 1, 2023.)

Translator's Notes

FICHTENBERG'S ORIGINAL SAMPLES & OTHER IMAGES

Fichtenberg's 1852 book was bound with 32 sample swatches[1] pasted in after his last chapter. These samples measured just 3.5×2 cm and have been enlarged for this printing.

As noted in the image credit lines, all of the other examples in this edition have been taken from public domain sources.

POTASH

Potash is a general term that can be used to refer to a number of very different things. M. Fichtenberg was not always clear in his instructions and most often simply indicated to use *potash* rather than being more specific. Every effort has been made to clarify this in the translation when possible. For additional information, see the following table and POTASH in the SUPPLEMENTAL MATERIAL.

---

1   Specimens begin on page 163 of this edition.

POTASH

Word(s) used by Fichtenberg	IUPAC name and chemical formula	Synonyms
cream of tartar	Potassium (2R,3R)-2,3,4-trihydroxy-4-oxobutanoate $KC_4H_5O_6$	potassium bitartrate, potassium hydrogen tartrate, potassium acid tartrate, monopotassium tartrate, beeswing
pearl ash, potash, salt of tartar	Potassium carbonate K_2CO_3	carbonate of potash, dipotassium carbonate, sub-carbonate of potash, salt of wormwood
yellow prussiate of potash	Potassium hexacyanidoferrate(II) $K_4[Fe(CN)_6] \cdot 3H_2O$	potassium ferrocyanide
caustic potash	Potassium hydroxide KOH	lye, potash lye, potassia, potassium hydrate
	Potassium sulfate K_2SO_4	potassium sulphate, sulphate of potash, potash of sulfur

OTHER

Word(s) used by Fichtenberg	IUPAC name and chemical formula	Synonyms
alumina	Aluminium oxide Al_2O_3	aluminium(iii) oxide, dialuminium trioxide
muriatic acid	Chlorane HCl	hydrochloric acid, spirits of salt
nitric acid	Nitric acid HNO_3	aqua fortis, spirit of niter, eau forte, hydrogen nitrate, acidum nitricum

OTHER

Word(s) used by Fichtenberg	IUPAC name and chemical formula		Synonyms
quicklime	Calcium oxide	CaO	lime, burnt lime, unslaked lime, free lime (building), caustic lime, pebble lime, calcia, oxide of calcium
sal ammoniac	Ammonium chloride	NH_4Cl	salammoniac, salmiac
tin salts	Tin(IV) chloride	$SnCl_4$	tin tetrachloride or stannic chloride

PIGMENTS

Word(s) used by Fichtenberg	Description/Source	Synonyms
Cassel earth brown, Vandyke brown	Obtained from peat or soil from Kassel, Germany (called *Cassel* until 1926)	Vandyke brown, Cassel earth, Castle earth, Cologne earth, Kassel brown
gallnuts	Tannin found in the gall is used as a black ink or dye.	oak apple, oak gall
Caput mortuum [referring to a brown color—not the purple version]	Rich brown color. Historically made from the flesh of mummies mixed with white pitch and myrrh.	mummy brown, Egyptian brown
Quercitron	Obtained from the bark of the Eastern Black Oak (*Quercus velutina*) tree indigenous in North America	formerly called Dutch pink, English pink, or Italian pink

PIGMENTS

Word(s) used by Fichtenberg	Description/Source	Synonyms
stil de grain, Avignonberries Persian seed	derived from berries of the buckthorn species *Rhamnus saxatilis*.	French berries, Persian berries lake, yellow berries, buckthorn berries. This yellow color was formerly called pink (or pinke), Dutch pink, brown pink, English pink, Italian pink, or French pink

ROSINS/RESINS

Word(s) used by Fichtenberg	Description/Source	Synonyms
Balsam of Tolu	derived from *Myroxylon balsamum var. balsamum*	Tolu balsam
benzoin [resin]	balsamic resin from several species of trees in the genus *Styrax*	gum benjamin, Sambrani loban, storax
colophane rosin	resin obtained from pines	colophony, Greek pitch
copal varnish	aromatic resin, especially from the copal tree *Protium copal*	
dragon's blood	resin from different species including *Calamus rotang, Croton, Dracaena* and *Pterocarpus*.	
gum arabic	gum consisting of the hardened sap from *Senegalia senegal* or *Vachellia seyal*.	gum acacia, gum sudani, Senegal gum

ROSINS/RESINS

Word(s) used by Fichtenberg	Description/Source	Synonyms
liquid styrax	"The genuine liquid Styrax is, even at Moco, a very rare commodity, and sold at a very high price, and it has seldom entered the shops of our apothecaries. A resinous juice, possessing somewhat of the same sensible qualities, brought from the Spanish provinces of South America, and perhaps the product of the same tree, is sometimes sold in place of it. But much more frequently what we meet with under this name, is an artificial compound of solid storax, common resin, wine, and oil, beat up together, to a proper consistence."[2]	*ungmentum e stryace,* mitia, cotter-miza, roca-mahla, false aromatic storax
mastic	resin from *Pistacia lentiscus*	tears of Chios
sandarac	resin from *Tetraclinis articulata*	sandarach
Venetian turpentine	a resin is derived from the sap of the deciduous *Larix decidua, Pinaceae*	Venice turpentine resin, balsam of Venice turpentine

2 https://www.ncbi.nlm.nih.gov/pmc/articles/PMC5650834/pdf/medphysj74043-0055.pdf. Retrieved September 27, 2023.

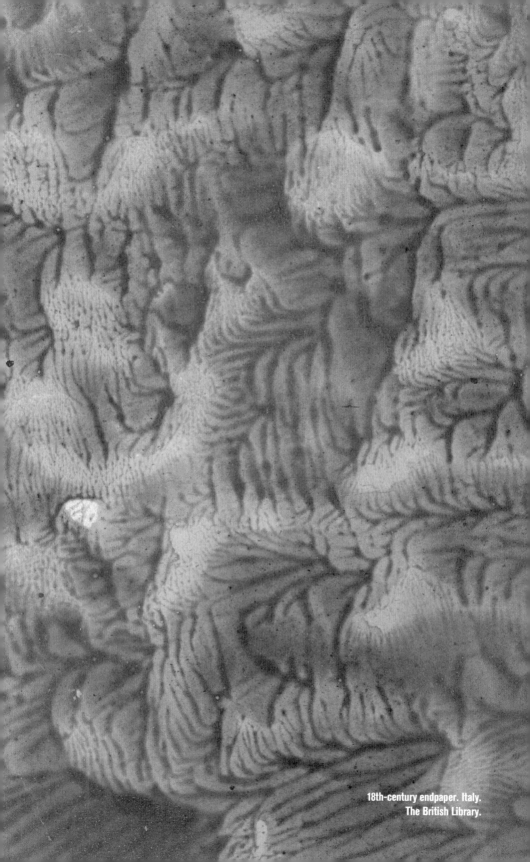

18th-century endpaper. Italy.
The British Library.

FICHTENBERG'S GUIDE
TO MAKING FANCY PAPER

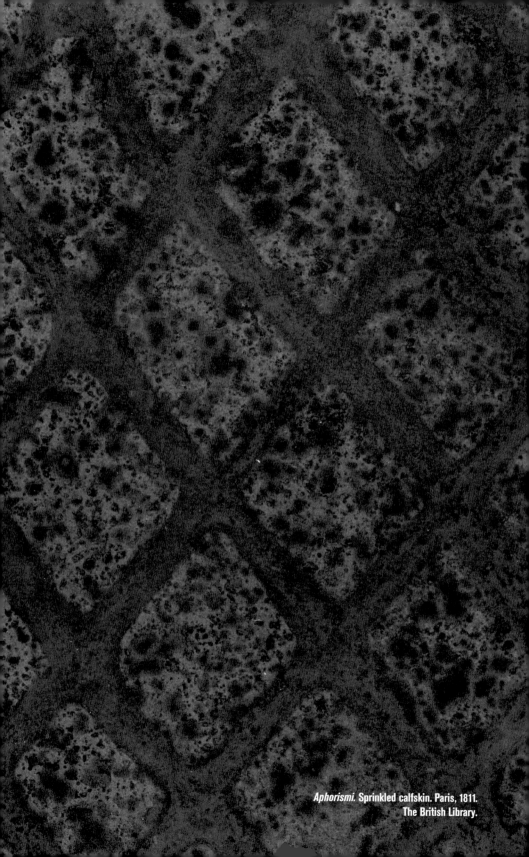

Aphorismi. Sprinkled calfskin. Paris, 1811.
The British Library.

Preface

The art we will try to describe precisely is generally little known, although it is ancient. Its history is obscure, incomplete, and uncertain and of little importance to the manufacturer and the amateur; for these reasons, we will not try to trace its various phases here and proceed immediately to the descriptions of the methods it involves.

These methods are generally highly varied, most highly ingenious and almost entirely due to the practice of the workshops. One must have been a manufacturer; one must have worked in the various types of which this industry is composed as a whole to know them all thoroughly, describe them and recommend them. It is an advantage that I had (and that will be helpful to me as a recommendation to the benevolence of the reader), especially when he knows that I have practiced these various methods for more than thirty years in France and Germany—true homelands of fancy papers—and countries where they are still manufactured with the highest taste, the greatest variety, and tremendous success.

Therefore, in this Manual, I have recorded the facts I have collected in my practice and all those that a long industrial career has enabled me to observe in the workshops of other manufacturers. Most of the formulas I have given are known only to people in the trade. Technicians have not collected and published them, either because they were forbidden to enter the workshops, because they were left unaware of the tricks of the trade, or because these elegant and graceful industries were thought to be of too little importance to merit serious attention on their part.

I will dare to say, however, that this modest manufacture is worthy of the attention of the observer; that it does not, it is true, put into practice beautiful operations or great chemical reactions, but that it has been able to employ a host of physical means whose observation certainly indicates a sagacity, and, I will even say, a genius that would do honor to our professional physicists and academics.

Thus, the manufacturer of fancy papers has been applying and taking advantage of, for a considerable time, the laws of color contrast, the curious phenomena of capillarity, the physical laws of attraction, repulsion, the mobility of liquids, their physical affinities, their incompatibilities, the effects of pressure and flow of fluids, their superposition, those of the brush, the sponge, etc., in its innumerable products marbled, flowed, scraped, wood, quilted, jaspered, moirés, satin, etc., etc. We, manufacturers, have been content to observe these phenomena and make use of them. However, skilled physicists visiting our workshops would still find some new subjects worthy of study that we will not allow ourselves to point out in our humble position.

The manufacture of fancy papers is, as we have said, a modest industry and one in which formidable competition significantly reduces profits; it often happens, therefore, that those who engage in this manufacture also carry on some other small industry connected with it; this is what has prompted us to describe these industries, according to the findings of our own practice.

The first of these industries we address is metallic papers, used today in manufacturing notebooks, portfolios and binding works. We attach some importance to this process, which was never described before and is indebted to us for several improvements.

We then move on to the Congrève's printing process—the means of which has never been described in sufficient detail—which we have partly imported into France and which are also indebted to us for some progress. We describe the way we have practiced it in Paris for many years.

We then proceeded to describe the manufacture of sealing wax, not according to the formulas found in books, but according to those modified and made necessary by the consumers' taste, the fair market, and the competition.

Another piece of art, the description of which had remained almost unpublished, is the manufacture of lead pencils and the apparatus used for this purpose. We hope, in this respect, to have given a complete description of this industry, which we have practiced for a long time in Paris.

The formulas for the current manufacture of pastels had scarcely been published, primarily because modern chemistry has provided the manufacturer with new and wonderful colors or that it has elevated, by skillful manipulations, the tone and nuance of the old ones. We guarantee the ones we present in this Manual as proven by our experience.

Finally, we have grouped together in this Manual some additional industries, such as the glazing of papers and prints, the manufacture of sealing wax, mouth glue, colored inks, shoe polish, sandpaper, and rubber tablets, etc., which an amateur could even practice himself based on the precise instructions that we present.

We repeat, in conclusion, that the descriptions and formulas we give in this Manual are all the fruit of practice and experience. It is possible to do differently, and it is also possible to do better. Still, after long practice, we are convinced that our methods, properly implemented, lead to good results.

We wanted to make known various elegant and fancy arts that can be practiced for profit or as an amateur. We would be happy if the approval of the public were granted to us for having tried to make it know about some practices and to have put it in possession of some methods which have been, until now, secrets of the factory and workshop.

Introduction

The use of fancy papers is very substantial, either for bookbinding or for cardboard; they are also used for a host of other purposes that we will have the opportunity to mention. The art of making them is not complex, and entire families can find a salary and profits in this industry because there is work for all ages, all strengths and all intelligences. We will present here the description of the processes proper to manufacture each kind so that there is not a bookbinder or a cardboard maker using these papers who cannot make some himself for his use and at little expense.

Marbled paper has been known for several centuries. It was mentioned in a chemistry book printed in 1694, but this ancient document did not offer much on the variety of the patterns, and only one type was described. For the last 30–40 years, the art has made significant progress in the elegance and refinement of the patterns and the quality of the glazing. Even today, there are very few manufacturers who can make all the varieties. Because particular chemical processes or physical effects decorate these papers, the manufacturer can maintain his secrecy indefinitely. Marbled papers are manufactured in several countries, notably in England and Germany, and each manufacturer or inventor has applied a name to each type that he first introduced.

German papers have always been preferred because of the variety of patterns, beautiful smoothness, and glossy finish. They are known as *fire varnish*, a name given to it because of the brilliance that this varnish gives. The English have always preferred and retained the shaded or combed patterns.

There are several factories in Germany: Prussia, Saxony, Offenbach, Darmstadt and Aschaffenburg. Messrs. G. Wuste, in Darmstadt, and Dessauer, in Aschaffenburg, have the reputation of being skillful manufacturers, especially the latter, which has one of the most robust factories in the world. There is a place called Neustadt on the Harte, where almost all the inhabitants only owe their livelihood to the manufacture of ordinary paper, plain and printed colors, and Indian printed paper, the products of which find a very considerable distribution in the colonies. In Nuremberg and Augsburg (Bavaria), many papers are coated with imitation gold; images of saints, birds, etc., are also printed with this imitation gold. These prints and designs are, it seems, the most important. These prints and designs are, it is true, crude but cheap; the production is very significant, especially in the latter city, which sends large deliveries to all parts of the world.

The Germans are also famous for the manufacture of leatherette papers, which they know how to give a lovely grain and a shiny finish that does not need wax to be polished. The same texture is produced in France, but the finish is not yet well known. In Saxony, especially in Dresden, they make well-varnished ground papers with a great variety of designs and colors.

Marbled papers have been manufactured in France for a long time but with very ordinary patterns. However, during the last 20–25 years, many improvements have been introduced. Today, we are successful with some patterns. If this industry spreads and receives the necessary encouragement, there is no doubt that France will be able to do better than any other nation.

M. F. M. Montgolfier, in Annonay, has invented an exquisite and highly valued marbled paper. This product is very-requested for the covers of the books and the ledgers. In Strasbourg, papers imitating agate are manufactured. These papers are also popular because of the variety of designs and because they perfectly mimic the natural agate.

As for the other so-called fancy papers—satin, moiré, embossed, printed either with the woodblock or lithographic stone, gold, silver, and any other luxurious paper—France will always retain its monopoly and will remain masters of this art.

Since lithography has made such remarkable progress, and one can print papers by this method, one does not need to use woodblocks as much as before. Woodblock prints are not as beautiful, as sharp, and as crisp. Because one cannot be sure of the inks' distribution or charge, sometimes one loads more color than is necessary. This causes an impression with unevenness, especially with gold. The use of a thick mordant, which spreads the colors at the time of impression, makes that impression increasingly coarse and lacking in sharpness. I propose to indicate a coating with which one can print very cleanly, which will dry immediately, especially for bronzes, which can be smoothed and gives a more brilliant paper than gold in sheets.

Each manufacturer must know how to prepare the colors he uses for his purposes because it is always better to use the best colors, even when they are more costly, if you want to obtain the most beautiful results and wish to spend less. In the trade, one sometimes finds useless colors because the manufacturer has added too much filler, which is pointless. After all, if one wants to do ordinary work, one can add as much filler as one desires to high-quality colors. In Paris, one can still find good colors, but it is more difficult in the provinces. In this case, everyone can easily make the colors he needs at little cost—even in small batches.

To make this publication as helpful as possible to paper makers, bookbinders and manufacturers of fancy papers, I have tried to supplement it by including information on all the items used in these various professions and are necessary for them. Thus, following the information on colored papers, I have described the manufacture of translucent papers for tracing; imitation donkey skin; sealing wax; various sealing wafers; black ink; siccative varnishes; mouth glue; artificial slate; a good, cheap paste glue; and manufacture of metallic papers for English notebooks.

FANCY PAPER

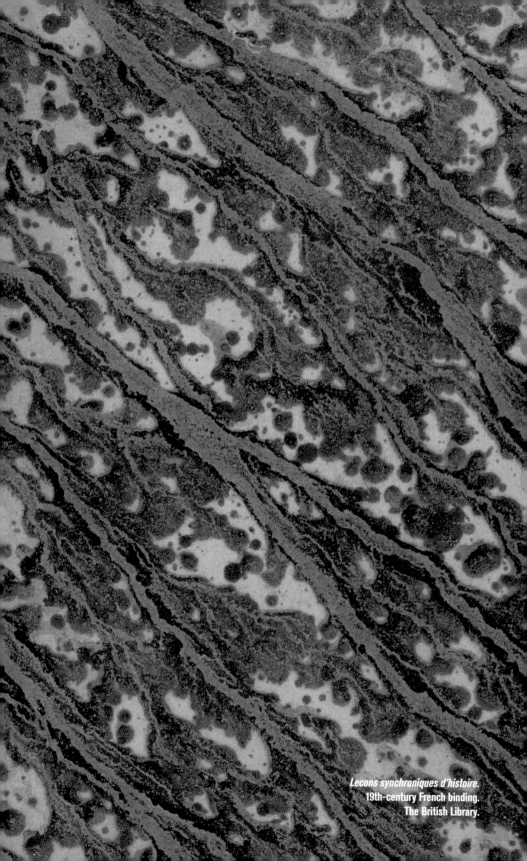

Lecons synchroniques d'histoire.
19th-century French binding.
The British Library.

Making the Colors

To make colors, it is necessary to have a heavily tinned copper boiler, the capacity of which will depend on the number of colors that you want to make at once. You will also need several sieves, barrels, jars, and other vessels to store, precipitate and wash the colors; cloths for filtering; grinding stones and wheels; a milling machine to work in large volumes; a mortar, etc.

Above all else, I recommend choosing the colors, salts, and acids wisely and buying only the best grades—even when the prices are very high—because these grades yield more value and provide more beautiful colors. It is also crucial to maintain extreme cleanliness throughout production. You must wash the utensils and vessels well each time you want to work with different colors. It is also essential to use only river water or rainwater, but if these are in short supply, you could use well water for cleaning, provided it is quite clear.

The colors necessary for the manufacturing of fancy papers are the following: carmine lake, red lake, yellow, violet, imitation blue and black, Berlin blue and Prussian blue, and fine chrome yellow. Then come other colors, some of which are natural and some that are the product of important industries that require large factories and capital. It is essential to obtain the best quality because, if necessary, it is better to mix them with whites or other substances than to buy them already mixed in unknown proportions and with unknown substances.

The natural colors are yellow earth, yellow Italian earth, Cassel [Vandyke] brown, calcined Italian earth, and gall nut.

The manufactured colors are vermilion, orange lead, ultramarine, ceruse white, flake white, Schweinfurt green, fine blue (called *Paris blue* or *ash blue*), washing soda, alkalies and alkaline salts, alum, vitriol, lead salts; and acids including nitric, muriatic and tartaric.

Imitation gold leaf comes from Nuremberg, Germany. There are many grades, of which there are always two sizes—large and small; the small size is more beautiful. That with the markings of Espermuller, J. Cospar Mayer, Fuchs, are the most used, but only for gilded papers; for other works, this kind is too heavy and cannot easily be used. It is then necessary to use that from Cubler, Linz. For ordinary works, one uses the large format of the same manufacturers, according to the price one wants to pay—the redder the gold leaf is, the less expensive it is. It is the same as with bronze powder; the price varies with the fineness; the grades range from № 10–2000. The shades are distinguished by the designations of English green, gold color, Paris, natural, orange, lemon, pale yellow, silver and imitation silver, and red carmine. It is always necessary to use the best grade because the more refined they are, the better results they deliver. The ordinary ones are often mixed with litharge [lead oxide]. The best colors are English green, gold color, and natural. If one wants to use several gold colors, one must use tones that contrast well: English green gold, lemon, etc. They also make both very fine and cheaper types of bronze in England, but they are made differently, making them heavier, coarser, and easily tarnished.

Before making colors, it is necessary to prepare all the items necessary for their manufacture, including the acids, the body and tin dissolution, and the utensils, especially the filter. This filter consists of a square frame of about 80 cm on a side (2½ ft square), to which the cloth filter is attached at the four corners and rests on a four-legged trestle. In factories where work is done on a large scale, a foreman or special worker occupies himself only with the preparation of the colors. In the case of a small manufacturer, a worker can use his time to do other things while waiting for the color to boil, but as soon as it boils, it is essential to attend to it, stir it, and monitor it, especially when producing lake colors. One must also be careful not to let it boil too long; otherwise, the color will take on a dirty hue.

§ I. Preparation of Alumina[1] to Give Body to the Colors

In a boiler, alum is dissolved in 10 parts of river water, and when it is perfectly dissolved, it is poured into a barrel high enough to prevent the effervescence from spilling over the rim when potash is added.

The boiler is then rinsed so that no alum remains, and half the weight of alum is taken from the potash, called *pearl ash*, which is then dissolved in 8–10 parts of water, removed from the fire, and left to rest. It often happens that the potash leaves a residue, but when it has settled the dissolution, it is poured into the barrel over the alum very gently and in a thin stream, constantly stirring with a stick, after which it is left to settle for ten to 12 hours; the liquid is clarified shortly afterward, and the alumina precipitates to the bottom.

The barrel must be pierced at various heights with several holes, which are to be plugged with pegs that can be pulled out as desired; when the peg above the precipitate is pulled, the excess water will flow out. The hole is plugged again, and the barrel is refilled with water; the barrel is agitated, left to rest, and the water is allowed to flow out, repeating this operation up to 5–6 times until the precipitate no longer has the slightest taste. What remains is then put on the screen to drain off all the water and put in a container to preserve it. It is essential to pour a little water on it so the alumina won't dry out and keep the container well-covered so that the powder does not become contaminated.

§ II. Tin Dissolution

Muriatic acid	3	parts
Nitric acid	2	—
Sal ammoniac	1	—
Water.	8	—

Muriatic acid and nitric acid are placed in sufficiently large bottles surrounded by a layer of straw. Pure drawn tin wire is added little by little until the acid is sufficiently saturated and no longer dissolves any more metal. This can be seen when the acid no longer gives off

---

1   *alumina*— aluminum oxide.

reddish fumes. The sal ammoniac, dissolved in water, is added little by little and left to stand.

§ III. Processes for Making the Colors
I. RED AND PURPLE COLORS

A. RED LAKES

№ 1. *Carmine Lake*

Take one part of cochineal, crush it on a mortar and pestle, not too fine, and put it on the fire in an extremely well-tinned pot with fifteen parts of filtered water. It is left to boil over a gentle fire for about twenty minutes, and a few minutes before being removed from the fire, white and pure cream of tartar (measuring one-third of the weight of the cochineal). The color takes on a yellow tone, and in this state, take it off the fire and add little by little as much volatile alkali [lye], which helps it take on a beautiful crimson color, and let it rest. It is necessary to take care not to put too much volatile alkali; otherwise, the color will turn purple. When the color is well settled, it is strained through a very fine sieve, and alumina is added depending on whether one wants to have a more or less beautiful lake. If one wants to have a beautiful color, it is precipitated with the dissolution of tin, and very little alumina is added. In all cases, one must be careful not to add too much alumina because the lake will become too pale. The residue that remains in the barrels is boiled again and processed, as explained above. But the lake thus obtained is more ordinary; in all cases, do not neglect the washes.

You can also precipitate this lake with the tin salts found in druggists' shops, so the color will take on a carmine tone. In this case, the precipitation is incomplete, so the remaining liquor is stored to precipitate with alumina and tin dissolution. This lake is very expensive and is not even used for fancy paper, except for those who make flower papers. I would even advise, if necessary, to buy carmine for this use because this operation is challenging: one must be skilled and practiced; otherwise, you won't be successful. One can purchase carmine lake from manufacturers at more moderate prices than it can be made; one can also buy (from leather makers) the residues of the colors they use to dye the hides. This color is very good for plain colored papers or leather, but it is too liquid for other applications. It can be thickened with starch diluted in cold water.

№ 2. Red Lake with Brazilwood

Place fifty parts of clear water (river water) in a tinned boiler on the fire with twelve parts of chopped brazilwood and two parts of alum. Boil the whole thing over low heat for a good half hour and then pour into a large barrel. (The barrel must have a large capacity because by precipitating the color, it rises and could overflow). Add alumina and a little tin dissolution, stirring constantly. When the color precipitates, stop and let it rest.

№ 3. Red Lake

Place fifty parts of water (always filtered river water) in a boiler; add three parts of alum and fifteen parts of chopped brazilwood. Let it boil for a good half hour over a gentle fire. Place a sieve on a large barrel with a capacity of at least double the volume of the liquid. This is done by placing two pieces of rounded wood on the barrel and placing a sieve on top for the color that is in the boiler; take care that no wood chips fall. When this is done, the potash you have dissolved is added drop by drop until the color precipitates. When everything has settled to the bottom, the water is decanted, and new water is added in the same way five or six times in a row. Finally, pour it over a strainer, and when all the water is drained, put it in a jar to preserve it. It is necessary always to pour a little water on this color; otherwise, it will dry or develop fungal growth.

Red lake can also be made using redwood from Sainte-Marthe [France] or other redwood in the same way as with brazilwood, but the lake is not as beautiful, and the best is always brazilwood. If you want to use it for common works, add starch diluted in cold water. Pass this starch, which you have mixed with the lake, through a sieve to mix it well. Using this method, you can make lakes as ordinary as you want; the more starch you add, the lower the quality of the lake.

B. VIOLET LAKES

№ 1. Purple Lake

Boil sixty parts filtered river water with four parts alum and twenty parts campeche wood in a tinned copper pot; after boiling for a good half hour, remove the liquid from the fire and pour it through a sieve into a large barrel; then add a solution of potash [potassium carbonate] little by little, constantly stirring the color until it no longer precipitates anything. After the color has been left to rest for 10–12 hours, decant the clear liquid and wash the color five to six times with pure water; pour it through a filter. The prepared lake is stored in containers and covered with a bit of water. This lake should not be stretched with starch because it is already quite cheap, but a little alumina can be added.

№ 2. Blue Violet Lake

River water	60	parts
Campeche wood	15	—
Alum	1	—
Cyprus vitriol (copper sulfate)	2	—
Alumina can be added		

№ 3. Violet Lake with a Bronze Tone

River water	60	parts
Campeche wood	15	—
Alum	3	—

Use the same method as for № 1, but precipitate with the tin solution and add a little muriatic acid. Do not change the water as many times as for № 1 because too much of the acid would be removed, and the color would lose its bronze tone. Also, be careful not to add too much muriatic acid; this violet lake is already quite corrosive, and the additional acid would burn the paper. (Quite often, it is not necessary to add any muriatic acid at all.) There is no need to use alumina. The maker can change the tone by adding a little tin salt, sal ammoniac or tartaric acid. Each of these chemicals will give the color a different tone.

II. YELLOW COLORS

The yellow colors used in the manufacture of fancy paper are yellow lake, stil de grain, light and dark chrome yellow, ochre, and Italian ochre. This last color has two types that are bought raw and purified by decanting and grinding. It can also be found prepared and ground, at a very moderate price, in the Paris trade, but it is more economical to make your lake, stil de grain, and chrome yellow.

A. YELLOW LAKES

№ 1. *Yellow*

Make a decoction with two parts of Avignon berries in 20–24 parts of water. Let it boil for about an hour; strain it through a fine sieve; put the mixture back on the fire and add four parts of potash or two parts of pure soda; this potash or soda must be melted and strained. The remaining residue is again boiled and precipitated with a hot alum solution—about twice as much as the potash or soda used. One part of calcium carbonate (Meudon white) is added, creating a paste called *stil de grain*. For this to work properly, the powder must be well mixed and added at the same time as the precipitate. When all the alum color has precipitated to the bottom, change the water several times and filter. Adding alumina is unnecessary, but it is possible to add a little white clay (pipe clay well washed and clarified).

№ 2. Yellow

Put in a boiler:

Chopped yellow wood	5	parts
Quercitron	5	—
Alum	2	—
Water	30	—

Boil for a good half hour, remove from the fire, draw off and precipitate with potash and a little tin solution, adding alumina to give more body; wash five to six times, filter, etc.

These are the two yellow lakes that are best suited for making paper. Since these lakes are mainly used for green colors, no white matter other than alumina should be added.

B. CHROME YELLOW

This color, with its rich tone and good coverage, is the most suitable for making yellow papers, and its low price allows it to be used for the most ordinary kinds of work. It is not quite as useful for making green because it scarcely yields anything but dirty tones.

The manufacture of chrome yellow is easy; it only requires care and attention to obtain the desired shades. There are two kinds of potassium chromate: *yellow chromate* and *red chromate*. One must take care that these chromates are pure and that their crystals are shiny, brittle, and dry.

PREPARATION
№ 1. Canary Yellow

Using twelve to fifteen parts of cold water in a barrel, dissolve one part potassium chromate. Add 2½ parts soda ash [washing soda]. At the same time, dissolve lead acetate, also cold. The lead acetate is poured drop by drop into the *potassium chromate* until a beautiful yellow color is produced and the overlying liquor becomes clear. Then, two to four parts of starch diluted in cold water are mixed in and immediately poured through the filter. When the water is drained, more is poured in, and so on, for two or three days.

№ 2. Lemon Yellow

Dissolve one part of *red potassium chromate* in 18–20 parts of cold water, then precipitate with lead acetate (also dissolved in cold water); add three to four parts of starch diluted in cold water and wash and filter as before.

№ 3. Gold Color

This is done the same way as № 2, but instead of dissolving in cold, dissolve and precipitate hot. The hotter the dissolutions, the better the gold color produced; however, the starch must always be diluted in cold water and added to the precipitate when it is almost cold; otherwise, it will stick. The color takes on a red tinge by adding alkali—either lime water, soda, or potash. A beautiful red chrome color, almost as bright as vermilion and redder than orange lead, can be precipitated with *mercury nitrate* instead of *lead acetate*. Still, this color is expensive, yields little precipitate, and has no starch added.

III. BLUE COLORS

A. PRUSSIAN BLUE

Prussian blue, or *Berlin blue*, is a very beautiful blue—bright and dark—developed at the beginning of the eighteenth century in Berlin. Its manufacture later reached the four corners of the world. It is produced at specialized factories on a large scale. In these large factories, it is made from stone, but for the last thirty to forty years, a salt called [yellow] *prussiate of potash* has been prepared that is sufficient for producing a blue in a paste form that is more suitable for making colored paper than that made from stone. We will, therefore, only give the manufacturer of blue paste here.

PREPARATION

№ 1. Prussian Blue Paste

Take a stoneware jar having at least three times the capacity of the volume of the acids to be used. Add three parts of nitric acid to two parts of muriatic acid. Add very small amounts of iron oxide (copperas) and stir it from time to time with an iron rod until the acid is well saturated; that is to say, it no longer smokes. It is then left to settle; the liquid is drawn off into a large bottle and kept for use.

When adding iron oxide to acids, one must be careful to add it only in small pinches and at intervals of five to six minutes between each; otherwise, it will expand and cause the liquid to spill over.

To make blue, take fifty to sixty liters of water and dissolve two to three kilograms of [yellow] *prussiate of potash* in a copper or iron boiler. Put this solution in a barrel with a capacity of 100 liters, then carefully add the acid and iron solution (which has been kept in the bottle and shaken well before use) drop by drop and constantly stir with a stick or a wooden spatula. This process will cause the precipitate to take on a green color that will soon turn blue. The process is stopped as soon as it is seen that the liquid becomes clear and separates. For this purpose, a test is carried out by taking a square of gray paper without glue and forming a filter into which a little liquid is put in order to judge whether it flows clearly. If it does, the barrel is filled with water, left to stand for ten to twelve hours, and then the liquid is drained off.

For the second washing, one part of sulfuric or muriatic acid is added to twenty parts of water, adding to the brightness of the blue. This color is extremely dark—maybe even too dark for use. To lighten it, add a part of the alumina by precipitating. In this form, it is more convenient to use and covers better.

№ 2.

Put in a large stoneware vase in the open air:

Muriatic acid	5	parts
Nitric acid	3	—

Take iron filings that do not contain copper, zinc, or sandstone—impurities that are sometimes mixed with them to give them more weight. Add them to the acids little by little until it no longer smokes. Leave them to settle for a few days, stirring from time to time with an iron rod. To make blue, take six parts of [yellow] prussiate of potash and two parts of alum and dissolve them in 25–30 parts of river water. At the same time, put six parts of alumina in a large barrel and knead it with water until it forms a kind of paste. Then, pour a solution of prussiate of potash on this paste—constantly stirring—and add some dissolution of iron until a beautiful blue precipitates. When pouring the iron solution, constantly stir with the rod so it is thoroughly mixed. The first water is decanted and replaced by sulfuric acid diluted with 20 times its weight in water. It is left for four to six days, after which it is decanted, washed with pure water and filtered. This color, named *steel blue*, is coppery and very beautiful.

B. MINERAL BLUE

Take 5 kg (10 lb.) of Prussian blue paste № 1, to which alumina has been added and which has dried out. Put it in a boiler and dilute it with water. Add 1 kg (2 lb.) of pulverized alum. Let it boil for 1–1½ hours over low heat. Pour it into a barrel filled with water. When the color has settled, it is drawn off and washed several times until it no longer has the astringent taste of alum, after which 4, 5, 6, or even more parts of starch are added to the blue precipitate; more water is poured in, left to settle, drawn off and washed.

C. NEW BLUE—IMITATION ASH BLUE

Take 5 kg (10 lb.) of blue paste № 1, containing alumina and re-dried by weight, dilute it in water and mix with it a dissolution made with 250 grams (half a lb.) of potash. The color will take on a grayish tone. It is necessary to take care that the hue is not too gray and to stop immediately. At the same time, 125 grams (4 oz.) of tartaric acid are dissolved in water, and this dissolution is poured on the blue paste, constantly stirring. The color then turns light blue. Finally, add ½–1 kg (1–2 lb.) bismuth that has been diluted in water, and a very beautiful blue is obtained.

D. PARIS BLUE OR ASH BLUE

Dissolve some Cyprus vitriol (copper sulfate) in hot water or mix it with whitewash, which will give it a greenish color, and then some sal ammoniac powder until the paste turns blue. It is then covered very tightly. This color is very difficult to make; if it is left too exposed to the air, then the volatile alkali that is formed in contact with the lime from the whitewash and the sal ammoniac will evaporate, and the color will lose its brilliance. If the quantities are not observed precisely, either more or less, the color will not be successful. In this case, buying it from people who are used to such operations is better than making it yourself.

The paper manufacturer can replace this color with the previous one or mineral blue that has been washed with potash water and tartaric acid, at least for the first coat.

IV. GREEN COLORS

Green colors are generally based on blue and yellow. The desired shades can be made by mixing a yellow lake with mineral blue. For blueish shades, add more blue; for a more yellowish shade, add more yellow lake. A lovely green can also be created by adding chrome yellow with mineral blue leached with potash and tartaric acid. This produces a very beautiful green that provides a lot of coverage but with a hue that is not as pleasing as those made with lake yellow. Never use blues that are too dark.

Schweinfurt green and Scheele's green can also be used. These colors are too dangerous to make. It is best to buy them ready-made; nevertheless, we will give the procedures for their manufacture here.

A. SCHWEINFURT GREEN

This green, invented by [Wilhelm] Satler in Schweinfurt, surpasses all existing greens in beauty and clarity. Its use is widespread, but, as I have already said, its manufacture is very dangerous, and great care must be taken because of its arsenic.

Heat 6–7 kg (12–14 lb.) of verdigris in 15 liters of water in a copper boiler until the whole is dissolved into a paste. Dregs form and are washed by pouring vinegar into the paste. Pass it through a very fine sieve. Clean the boiler and add 25–30 liters of river water and 5–6 kg (10–12 lb.) of very finely pulverized white arsenic. Leave it to boil for two to three hours. Filter it through a cloth. The mixture is put back into the boiler, and when it is boiling, the verdigris solution is carefully poured in little by little because of the effervescence it causes. When all is poured in, boil until the color is pure and clear, then decant. (Often, some arsenic remains and is kept for the next operation). To obtain a brighter color, vinegar should be used instead of water to dissolve the verdigris; then wash and filter. One could also take, instead of verdigris, copper sulfate and dissolve arsenic acid with an equal part of potash. The process is the same as the previous one. The first washing is done with vinegar, but one should not use too much of it; otherwise, verdigris will form again.

B. SCHEELE'S GREEN[2]

Scheele's green is made in much the same way as Schweinfurt green, except that copper sulfate is used and slightly more potash than arsenic is used. Also, no vinegar is used. This color does not have as much brilliance as the previous one and easily turns to a yellowish tone.

There are many green colors of this sort, but paper manufacturers do not use them, so we thought it unnecessary to describe their

---

2   Scheele's Green was invented by Carl Wilhelm Scheele in 1775.

fabrication. The rest of the colors used in the manufacture of fancy papers are natural. Most of them are earth colors:

- yellow ochre,
- Cassel earth brown [Vandyke brown],
- Italian red ochre, and
- Italian yellow ochre.

These are all natural colors that must be bought in their raw form to be sure they are unadulterated. Among the other colors we will mention—those that have been manufactured—are vermilion, orange lead, ceruse white, silver white, etc. When purchased already ground, the latter is often stretched with ceruse white, even with quartz or various substances. Generally, it is better to have a worker in your shop who can grind, as they will be more beautiful colors and provide more value. One usually has a grinding machine with three, five, or even seven rollers or mills, like those for mustard. One can grind colors on a slab with a muller in small establishments. As for the earth colors, they need to be thoroughly processed into a paste before being used.

Hide Glue, Paste Glue, and Glazing Paste

§ I. Hide Glue

Take trimmings from white skins, rabbit skins, or hare skins, buying the latter two from people involved in fur cutting for the millinery industry. A flat tray of a size proportionate to the quantity of glue to be made is used. A layer of skins or trimmings 5–8 cm (2–3 in.) thick is placed in this tray and sprinkled with a coating of powdered quicklime[1] about 4–5 mm thick, and another layer of skins, then more lime, and so on until the tub is three-quarters full. Pour water over it until the skins are covered. Leave it in this state for ten to fifteen days, checking from time to time, and if the water has been absorbed, more is added. When the skins are well-softened, and one wants to make the glue, take a pot and put enough straw in the bottom, so it is well covered with it for a depth of about 10 cm (4 in.). Add water to the softened skins until half of the pot is filled. Put it on the fire and let it boil, skimming often until the skins are dissolved. Pour everything through a fine sieve into another tub and let it cool. It is good to point out that one should not make too much glue at once, especially in hot weather, and prepare only what can be used within six to eight days at most. In cold weather, it keeps longer. It is also necessary to pay attention that when one does not have any white skin trimmings, one

---

1   *powdered quicklime*—Calcium oxide

must use more lime, and on the contrary, if one has only trimmings of white skins, use only a little lime. Some manufacturers do not use any lime at all.

§ II. Paste Glue

Take good white flour (it doesn't need to be of the brightest whiteness, but it must be free of bran). Put it in a tub, pour water on it, and beat it until it is a thick paste, but be careful that the flour paste is not too dry. This often happens when too much water is added at the beginning. In the meantime, water is poured into a pot and put on the fire. When the flour is well beaten, boiling water is poured into it with a large saucepan, at first in small quantities and constantly stirring so that the paste remains uniform. It can be poured faster until the paste becomes lighter and more transparent. Stop and let it cool down. A skin will form on the surface. Cut it open at the edge when you want to use the paste; take the quantity you need, and recover it with the skin so that it will preserve itself. This paste is still better three or four days after making it. It is good to have more boiling water than you need for the paste because some flours absorb much more water than others.

§ III. Glazing Paste

It is necessary to have two types of glazing paste; the first is used for ordinary papers—namely plain or jaspered backgrounds; the second is used for satin-like papers, marbled papers, etc.

№ 1. [*Referred to later as* WAX AND SALT OF TARTAR[2].] Half a kilogram (1 lb.) of good white flour is dissolved in 2–3 liters of water. Then, 400–450 grams (12–15 oz.) of yellow wax that has been cut into small pieces is mixed in, placed on a low fire and boiled until the wax is melted, then it is allowed to cool. If the paste is too thick, add a little water while boiling; if it is too thin, a little flour slurry is added.

---

2   *salt of tartar*—potassium carbonate

Put on the fire, in a pot, 1½ liter of water with 60 grams (2 oz.) of salt of tartar. When the solution boils, add 500 grams (1 lb.) of white wax and boil until everything is melted, stirring often; then, let cool. This glazing paste can be kept for a long time.

№ 2. [*Referred to later as* SOAP AND WAX.] Melt one part of white Marseilles soap in rain or river water, and when the soap is well melted, add two parts of white wax, let it boil, remove from the fire and stir from time to time until the glazing paste is cooled.

Using first-quality white wax is unnecessary, but it must be pure and without additives. Yellow wax should not be used because it is greasier and does not melt as well.

How to Make Fancy Papers

The manufacture of fancy papers is a very broad industry divided into many specialties, of which the most important is the manufacture of marbled papers. The diverse patterns of this paper are applicable, as it is known throughout the world, to bookbinding, pasteboard and wrapping. Perhaps no type of fancy paper is more attractive and more pleasurable to produce than these papers. Chemical processes or reactions create all these patterns, and if the person who makes them has good taste and some knowledge of chemistry, he can invent new designs every day. Besides, manufacturing is relatively easy. It is only necessary to be very careful that the colors are maintained in the proper state and to take care of the cleanliness of the mucilages. The patterns can be varied infinitely by changing the colors for the veins or the backgrounds, making the pattern larger or smaller, using colors prepared for German papers for the veins, and using colors for English patterns as backgrounds, etc. One will see later when we begin to describe the production details, the potential of the art and the advantages one can draw from it.

§ I. Description of the Marble Paper Workshop

The workshop should be well-ventilated but without a cross-flow of air so that one sheet will not stick to the other. It should be large enough and high enough to hold about two reams of paper. You can then make a layout and reserve enough space to freely move around, at least on two sides, i.e., on one side and at the back, and at the same time, keep a space of 1½ m (5 ft.) square to do the work. Suppose the room is 6–7 m in two directions (18–21 ft.) and 4 m high (12 ft.); you then take cleats measuring 6–7 cm square (2–3 in.), which are nailed at distances of 60–98 cm apart (2–3 ft.), against the wall, over a length of about 3½ m (11 ft.). Then, fix on the opposite wall, at about 3½ m distance (11 ft.), stronger cleats; inside these cleats, as well as on those fixed to the wall, nail slats about 65 cm in height (2 ft.). On these boards, attach slats measuring about 3 cm (1 in.) high by 5 cm wide (2 in.) to form runners; these slats must be wider than high because when the stretcher is loaded, it could bend in the middle and fall if it does not rest sufficiently on the supports.

Frames are then built, and for this purpose use slats 3 cm wide (1 in.) exactly the length of the distance between two runners; then take long pieces of wood measuring 5–6 cm in width (2–3 in.) and 80 cm (30 in.) in length, to which you fasten the slats well and solidly, using perfectly squared tenons, and joined so that they slide well in the frames. In this way, twenty sashes and five runners are formed; the layout is then complete, and when it is full, it can hold two reams of paper. The sashes are placed inside the uprights and on the floor to be used as needed. If the workshop is 6–7 meters in all directions (18–21 ft.), then there will remain 1½ m (5 ft.) of space available on each side and sufficient space behind.

A drip tray is made from a 25–30 cm (10–12 in.) wide wooden board, shaped into a point at the front, about 6–7 cm (3 in.) long. This board is edged with other wood to a height of about 4 cm (2 in.), leaving only an opening or the extreme tip without edging so that the mucilage flowing from the sheets can easily pass through. This drainer should rest and be fixed on three legs, the one at the back being higher than those at the front. A large bowl or flat tub is placed in front of the tip of this board to receive the draining liquid.

At the front of the workshop, opposite the drying rack, place four 65 cm (2 ft.) wide trestles high enough for the marbler. These trestles are arranged so that a rectangular washtub 1 m (3 ft.) long by 65 cm (2 ft.) wide and 8 to 10 cm (3 to 4 in.) deep can be placed on two of them; a second washtub is likewise placed on the other two trestles, leaving enough space between the two washtubs for a table to hold four 25–28 cm (8–10 in.) diameter bowls.

A 65 cm (2 ft.) square board should be placed at each end of the table to hold the paper and sticks. Alternatively, you can have just three trestles and lay boards of sufficient length to accommodate the tubs, colors, papers, and sticks. One of two tubs can be one for the large-size papers and the other for smaller ones.

In a workshop where not much paper is produced, a single tub is sufficient. This tub must be large in size. One of the planks is exactly the length of the tub, and the other the width of a square sheet of paper. In this way, a tub is formed for square paper. This operation is also performed when the tub is filled with mucilage: the space filled with mucilage must also be covered to prevent the color from dripping into it.

If it is possible to have a table for preparing colors in the same room, stock that space with the colors and acids that will be required. On the side, put small nails with hooks to hang the brushes, sieves, etc., because it is always better that brushes are hung freely; otherwise, they may become damaged.

You need several broom straw brushes: small ones for the veins and larger ones for the backgrounds; small hog's bristle brushes for stirring the colors; different sieves 20–25 cm (6–7 in.) in diameter for filtering the colors; bowls of the same diameter for the vein colors, and 40–45 cm (15–18 in.) for the background colors; several pieces of wood, rounded on one side and flat on the other, to put on the bowls. When you want to filter the colors, you place two similar sticks, with the flat side on the bowl and the sieve on the round side, so that the color doesn't stay on the wood. You must have an assortment of these sticks so a clean one can be used for each color. All these utensils must be kept clean and always washed with fresh water after use so that the color does not dry on them.

For the plain background papers used to make marbled papers, you need another space, which you arrange as follows: Get a square table, 2–3 m (6–9 ft.) long and 80 cm to 1 m (2½–3 ft.) wide, and not too high, so that a ream of paper can be placed on it, and the helper can easily move around it with his brushes. On this table, we place a board the size of the paper being used and, next to it, a large bowl about 60–65 cm (20–25 in.) in diameter. In this room, a string layout is set up. Two planks are nailed firmly to the walls, about 40–42 cm (15–16 in.) below the ceiling and equally close to its surface, one facing the other. On these two boards, hooked nails are fastened at intervals of 5–6 cm (2–3 in.), and strings are pulled over the hooked nails and tied so that air can circulate between the sheets. If the room is sufficiently lofty, you can make two rows of ropes, the second at the same distance below as the first is from the ceiling so that the sheets can't touch. In one corner, another table is set up to prepare the color, and if space is limited, this preparation can also be done on the same table used to make the backgrounds.

In the corner of the room, another table will be used to prepare the color, and if there is not enough space, this preparation can also be done on the same table used to make the backgrounds.

You also need two large bowls for the colors, a hog's bristle sieve, a little smaller than the bowls, a large brush for passing the color through the sieve, and round pieces of wood on one side and flat on the other to place the sieve on the bowl.

You'll also need a brush 15 to 16 cm (6 to 7 in.) long and 5 cm (2 in.) wide, made of soft hog's bristle, and a brush 18 to 20 cm (7 to 9 in.) in diameter for smoothing. These brushes are available from brush-makers in all sizes. There are also stretchers made with a rounded wooden stick, from 1.8 to 2 meters (5 to 6 ft.) long, to the top of which is fitted a thin crosspiece, 6 to 7 centimeters (2 to 3 in.) wide, which must be well united, attached by threading to the stick, the whole rounded and flat on each side, so that the stretcher does not catch on the cords. Place the color table in the middle of the room so there's space on the sides for any objects or equipment you may need.

§ II. Polishers

There are two kinds of polishers: those with a broad stone—called *French polishers*—for ordinary papers, and *German polishers*—with a round stone—for superior papers.

A. THE FRENCH POLISHER

Take a plank of fir wood, 3 m long (9 ft.), 24–33 cm wide (9–12 in.), and 4 cm thick (1½ in.). At one end of this board, about 8–10 cm from the end (3–4 in.), a hole of 3–4 cm in diameter is drilled. On this board are attached two flanges, i.e., two blocks of wood about 16–20 cm thick (6–8 in.) by 5–7 cm wide (2–3 in.). One of these flanges is nailed in the middle, and the other is nailed to the end of the board that is not drilled. Fasten these pieces of wood to the board on the ceiling firmly, and in this way, you get a board that makes a spring. Take a piece of wood rounded 4–5 cm (1½–2 in.) thick and with a length proportionate to the height of the piece. On this piece of wood, which is rounded, is made a base of about 10 cm (4 in.) high, by 5 cm wide (2 in.), and 16 cm (6 in.) long. In the height of this piece of wood, there is a rounded notch to fit the post, which must be rounded by the bottom, while the other end must enter the round made in the board against the ceiling to move the base from right to left. A notch should accommodate the polishing stone at the bottom of this base. This stone is a very pure black flint, without blemish, 5–6 cm wide (2–2½ in.), 16–18 mm thick, and 5 cm high (2 in.), thinned little by little towards the bottom, until it is only 5–6 mm thick, and rounded off. Use a sturdy table for polishing. On this, you put a board of well-leveled walnut wood that measures 65 cm by 80 (24–30 in.) and 5–7 cm thick (2–3 in.) so that this table is larger than the paper to be polished. The board that is placed on the ceiling should be about 33 cm (1 ft.) from the wall of the room. Attach a rope to the end and a hook on the wall, where you secure the said rope to give more or less load.

The polishing stone will often wear out. To restore its edge, use a hard wooden block that you put emery on. Grind the stone to give it a new edge.

B. THE GERMAN POLISHER

Use a plank of fir wood, 15–16 cm wide (5–6 in.), 5 cm thick (2 in.) and 2.65–3 m long (8–9 ft.). This board must also be attached to the ceiling at the top end and at a distance of 1–1.3 m (3–4 ft.) against the wall and on rods 10–12 cm thick (3–4 in.) so that there is a gap between the board and the ceiling. To make the front spring, the board is assembled using a strong hinge to another piece of wood, which is less wide and of a length proportionate to the height of the room where you work. This piece is of two pieces but joined with tongue and groove. The tongue and groove must be made in such a way as to be able to extend the piece and give the load through holes that are drilled at intervals; the end of the part bears a strong iron fitting in the shape of a fork and has strong brackets to clamp the polishing stone.

This polishing stone, which is an unblemished black flint, is round, about 10–12 cm in diameter (3–4 in.), 3 cm thick and rounded on each side. It rolls and slides in a pear wood groove that is fastened to the wooden table and is a little thicker than the stone.

§ III. Making Paper for Marbled Paper Backgrounds

This process is very easy; it offers no challenge, does not demand much attention and can be done by apprentices or women[1].

№ 1. *Pink Color*

In a bowl with a capacity of about 10 liters, put 3–4 kg of paste glue (6–8 lb.), three spoonfuls of glazing paste № 1, and 125 grams (4 oz.) of red lake (4 oz.). The mixture is beaten well and passed through a sieve into another bowl with river water until the color is fairly light and has the consistency of syrup. If you want it to be darker, add a larger proportion of red lake.

№ 2. *Light Red*

Paste glue 5	kg
Red lake 1½	—
Glazing paste № 1 4	spoonfuls
Water as needed.	

---

1 Keep in mind that Fichtenberg wrote this in 1852.

№ 3. Dark Red—Morocco Color

This color should not be too watery. The paper is given a layer of this color and a second layer of red № 2.

Orange lead	2½	kg
Paste glue	7½	—
Glazing paste № 1	5	spoonfuls
Water as needed		

№ 4. Light Yellow

Pale chrome yellow	1	kg
Paste glue	6	—
Glazing paste	4	spoonfuls
Water as needed, but not much		

№ 5. Deep Yellow or Golden Apple

Dark chrome yellow	1	kg
Orange lead	½	—
Paste glue	6	—
Glazing paste № 1	5	spoonfuls

These previous two yellow colors are bright; more matte yellows can be made when you take:

№ 6. Yellow

Take half a kg (1 lb.) of Avignon berries, boiled in 6–8 liters of water, and 125 grams (4 oz.) of alum. Lightly mix 6–7 kg (12–14 lb.) of paste glue and three spoonfuls of glazing paste № 1 with this liquid and let it cool.

№ 7. Yellow

Take 1½ kg (3 lb.) of yellow wood, half a kg (1 lb.) of turmeric powder, and 125 grams (4 oz.) of alum, boil with 12 quarts of water, and when drawn clear and allowed to cool, add 6–7 kg (12–14 lb.) of paste glue, and 3–4 spoonfuls of glazing paste.

№ 8. Brighter Yellow

Instead of alum, use 125 grams (4 oz.) of potash; the color will be more yellow and brilliant.

№ 9. Tan Color

Italian earth yellow, finely crushed in water . .	1	kg
Hide glue.	6	—
Glazing paste	5	spoonfuls

№ 10. Blue Color

This color can be made darker or lighter by adding more or less blue.

Prussian blue paste	½	kg
Paste glue	5	—
Glazing paste	3	spoonfuls

№ 11. Violet

Violet lake	1½	kg
Paste glue	5	—
Glazing paste	3	spoonfuls

№ 12. Lilac

Red lake	125	gm
Prussian blue paste	500	—
Meudon or Spanish white	1½	kg
Paste glue	7½	—
Glazing paste	6	spoonfuls

№ 13. Green

Boil 1 kg (2 lb.) Persian seed in 10 liters of water, with 125 grams of alum (4 oz.). When this liquid has cooled, add half a kg (1 lb.) of Prussian blue paste, 6 kg (12 lb.) paste glue, and five spoonfuls of glazing paste. It can be made more or less bright by putting more or less blue or yellow.

TO MAKE THE BACKGROUNDS

Lay a sheet of paper on the table as flatly as possible. The bowl containing the color is placed on the right side, and the brush is dipped into it and brushed over the paper, first lengthwise, then widthwise. The paintbrush is then put aside, and a dry brush is used to even out and spread the color. It is impossible to indicate here the amount of color that must be removed with the second brush, but you only need to do the work for one day to become perfectly skilled in this treatment.

When a sheet of paper has been covered with color, it is lifted by one of the corners between the thumb and index finger as soon as it has received the last brushstroke. It is laid onto a trestle placed beside the table until 20–25 sheets have been done. In this state, it is stretched on ropes, or if you have a helper, put the sheets directly on his hangar bar so that he can immediately carry them to the lines.

When the paper is quite dry, remove it from the lines. Straighten it and put it in a press to flatten it completely. It is essential for the marbling that the paper has an entirely flat and smooth surface; otherwise, it would create holes [paint voids]. As you can see, this operation is not difficult, and we believe it is unnecessary to dwell on it further.

§ IV. Making Marbled Paper

When the table has been arranged and the height of the table has been determined, two troughs are placed on it.

I. TROUGHS FOR MARBLING

The troughs are made of oak and must be large enough to hold two sheets of paper lying flat, either large or square, and 5–7 cm deep. These troughs are assembled with mortise and tenon joints. The bottom is slotted because it is constantly immersed in humidity; the wood swells, and in this way, it can be tightened with the wedge.

The troughs are placed on the table in such a way as to leave enough room to put paper and sticks at each end, and between the two troughs, four bowls of about 22 cm (8 in.) in diameter.

II. THE SIZE

To make marbled papers, two kinds of mucilage are used: first, that of gum tragacanth; second, that of psyllium seed, depending on the sort of marbling you want to produce.

A. PREPARATION OF THE SIZE

№ 1. Gum Tragacanth Size

Take a quantity of gum tragacanth, 2½–3 kg (5–6 lb.), for example, and place it in a round tub. (We usually use a wine barrel that has been sawn in half.) Pour river water over it and leave it for twenty-four hours; at the end, add water, agitate it, and leave it to rest until the gum is completely dissolved. The gum tragacanth does not dissolve but swells up until there is no single dry particle left. Once it is in this state, it is passed through a sieve and placed in another tub, with the addition of a few drops of alum water [made of 30 grams (1 oz.) of alum dissolved in a liter of water.] The mucilage is then complete.

We will point out here that fraud is widely practiced in the field of gum tragacanth. It is often mixed with spurious gum or a kind that comes from Aleppo. These kinds of gums, not being suitable for swelling, produce lumps and make the mucilage sour. It is, therefore, necessary to make sure of its good quality before buying it; it is also advisable to purchase only the very best quality. There is no need to pay attention to the color; often, the gum is yellow and gives the best mucilage. The flat, flakey gum is also preferable to the vermicular[2] type.

№ 2. Psyllium Size

Psyllium seed has the shape and appearance of a flea, which is why it is also sometimes called *flea seed*. This seed comes from the south of France and can be found at many herbalists, including Mr. Masson, rue de la Vieille-Monnaie. A kilogram of this seed can cost from 1 fr. 20 to 1 fr. 40. To make this psyllium mucilage, put a boiler that can hold 50–70 liters on the fire, fill it with water, and before it boils, prepare a barrel that can hold 200–250 liters, one end of which has been opened, and on which is fitted a sieve almost as big as the opening of the barrel. This sieve must be made of horsehair that is not too fine but tight enough so no seeds can pass through. Two square wooden bars are placed on the barrel so that the sieve rests firmly on it to prevent it from falling into the barrel when it is filled with seeds; otherwise, these seeds would mix with the mucilage and be very difficult to extract. When the water begins to boil, take 2–2 ½ kg (4–5 lb.) of psyllium seed and gently pour it into the water, always stirring carefully and taking care that the seeds do not drop too quickly into the water. Otherwise, they will clump up into a ball and no longer yield enough mucilage. (The seeds are slippery yet clump together easily.) When all the seeds have been poured into the boiler, stir a little more, but do not let the water boil. Remove the liquid little by little with a pot and pour it on the screen, adding constantly cold water in the boiler so that it does not boil. Use a big brush to rub the seed on the sieve to help the mucilage to pass.

When all the seed is removed from the boiler, it is put back for the second time so that with 2½ kg (5 lb.) of seeds, one can prepare 150–200 liters of mucilage. When it comes out of the boiler, the mucilage should be like a thick oil, and when it is cold, it should be very dense, so much so that it is sometimes necessary to cut it to remove portions.

2   *vermicular*—worm-like.

Having this mucilage prepared in advance is always essential, as it is too difficult to work with when it is fresh.

III. SUBSTANCES AND COLORS NEEDED
TO MAKE MARBLED PAPERS

1. Ox gall
2. Oils: walnut, rapeseed, poppy or other
3. Turpentine
4. White soap dissolved in river water
5. *Red American potash*, or better still *caustic potash* that is found at chemical manufacturers because people are often misled about the quality of commercial potash. Artificial potash is also manufactured, but it is stronger than American potash and not suitable for our use; it is easy to recognize it by the fact that the real American potash disintegrates in the air, and the artificial ones remain hard and solid and do not dissolve easily. One can use half a kg (1 lb.) of potash and half a liter of water because it is good to have very strong potash water so as to be able to add only a few drops. Let it settle well, and use only the clear liquid. You can add a little water if you notice that it is still too strong.
6. Glazing paste made with wax and soap
7. Alum water
8. Tartaric acid

All these substances should be prepared and ready in advance so that they are pure and clear and placed in narrow-necked bottles so that only a few drops can be dispensed at a time.

When you want to do some marbling, place the trough on the table. If you want to work with two, you need two troughs, and for some patterns, it is even necessary to have two troughs. The trough is loaded with one or the other of the mucilages described above, depending on the design you want to make. The following colors are used in this work:

1. Lampblack
2. Cassel earth [Vandyke brown]
3. Italian earth, yellow
4. Red lake
5. Violet lake
6. Yellow lake
7. Prussian blue
8. Chrome yellow
9. Berlin blue

All these colors must be in paste form, well-ground with water, and very fine.

IV. DIFFERENT MARBLED PAPERS
A. GERMAN MARBLED PAPERS

The German marbled papers offer the most variety of designs. To make these designs, one uses size № 1, № 2, or sizes № 1 and № 2 combined. Care should be taken not to use the size of the gum tragacanth design for the psyllium design because the pattern changes. A skilled worker can create new designs by mixing or changing the size.

The German marbled papers are referred to as:

1. Stone or Turkish
2. Partridge eye
3. Tiger marble
4. Schröetel
5. Large stone
6. Broken
7. Polish papers
8. Large champions

B. ENGLISH MARBLED PAPERS

There are only two patterns:

1. Shaded
2. Combed

C. FRENCH MARBLED PAPERS

There are two kinds: one invented by M. Montgolfier of Annonay; the other, called *agathe* paper, is made in Strasbourg, but this kind of paper is not made on mucilage.

A.   № 1. STONE OR TURKISH PAPERS
[*Papiers cailloutages ou turcs*]

PREPARATION OF MUCILAGE AND COLORS. Take mucilage № 2 (from psyllium seeds) in a bucket or large trough and cut it with water in proportion to its consistency. Beat it together or pass it through a sieve placed on the marbling trough on two wooden sticks until it is full. Agitate with care so that the bath is entirely homogeneous; it must be like syrup. Remove the foam and cover it with sheets of paper so the bath remains undisturbed. In the meantime, you prepare your colors.

Take a bowl whose size depends on the amount of paper to be made. In general, it is better to prepare more color than less because it will not spoil; however, when it is left too long, it will become dry, and then it must be reground and passed through a sieve.

The bowl should be thoroughly dry. For every half kg of paste color to be used, add 5–6 drops of one of the oils mentioned previously and a few drops of the soap solution. It is rubbed with a small brush the size of a finger. This work must be done diligently. Add a small amount of ox gall, little by little. When the bowl has been well rubbed and the mixture forms a white paste, the color is added little by little. Also, add a little of the glazing paste № 2 made from soap and wax, constantly rubbing, and then add some water until the color is sufficiently fluid, about the same as strong oil, and comes off easily from the brush. More ox gall is added, and everything is passed through a sieve into another bowl. The quantity of gall needed cannot be specified because some colors require more than others, and sometimes, moreover, one gall is stronger than another, so less must be added. The marbler can try his color; if it does not spread enough, he can add a little gall more easily than color.

Color	Brown	Vandyke brown
—	Yellow	Italian ochre
—	Pink	Red lake
—	Blue	Prussian blue
—	Violet	Violet lake
—	Black	Lampblack

For black, use lampblack from Germany or from Landes; the black from Paris is too light. You can mix German or Landes lampblack with so-called *German*, which comes from the area of Saarbrücken and costs about 60 centimes per kilogram, whereas lampblack costs 1.60 to 1.80 centimes.

One can make brown more yellow by mixing Italian ochre, or redder by adding red lake, and darker by adding black. Similarly, with purple, by adding red lake to purple lake, the color is more reddish, and with Prussian blue, it becomes lilac.

Make steel blue or gray by adding black to the purple lake.

Make green my mixing yellow lake and Prussian blue.

The paper should be placed on the edge of the trough, as well as the rods; the bowl of colors should be placed on a stool, and the brush on the bowl. A small brush is in the color to stir as needed.

The marbler then stands in front of the marbling trough. He removes the sheets of paper that have been covering the bath; to do this, he places a stick across the trough, throws half the sheet of paper over it and carries it to the stretcher so that the mucilage remaining on the sheet can run into the drainage tray indicated above. When this is done, he turns to the table where his color is, takes a little with the broom straw brush and lightly speckles it on the mucilage bath. The marbler will see immediately if the color expands enough, i.e., the color must be spreading in such a way as to become completely smooth and even without sinking. The drops must expand until they touch each other. If the color does not spread enough, it is necessary to add a little gall but be careful not to put too much at once, especially while you are still inexperienced. If it spreads too quickly, you must add more color. In either case, the color should be stirred with great care so that it is consistent.

The color now being in the proper state and the whole in good order, the marbler takes the paintbrush in the right hand, dips it in the bowl of color and tests to see if it is loaded with the correct amount—neither too much nor too little. One raises their left hand to chest level. Keeping the four fingers tightened and the palm turned towards the body, the hand stiffened and the thumb a little reversed, one then lifts the brush by the end of the handle and taps it on the bones that unite the fingers with the hand, that is to say on the first phalange. Tap about 3–4 cm (1 in.) from where the handle is inserted into the broom straw. Doing it this way will allow the color to come out of the brush very well. One must be careful that the drops fall evenly on the bath, and while striking, move back a little to achieve uniformity of the strokes. If one does not have enough color in the brush, start again, and when the bath is well-covered or loaded with paint, start again a second and even a third time, but with finer drops; this is the only way to obtain a beautiful marble.

Having done this, the marbler takes a sheet of paper with his hands in the middle of the sheet. With his right hand, he places the corner of this sheet in the corner of the trough and follows it with his left hand, rolling the sheet down onto the bath carefully so that it will not absorb too much color at once. Doing otherwise would trap air under the sheet and cause blank areas or grease spots to form, and in these places, the color would not stick to the paper.

When the first sheet is in place, a second one is worked on in the same way, taking the edge of the first sheet as a guide. The bath being thus covered with the two sheets, check that there are no air pockets, and if there are, tap on these places with a finger or make a few pinpricks with a needle so that the air escapes. Pull everything toward yourself in the trough with a finger to collect the color from the edge so that it attaches to the paper and does not mix with the mucilage; then put a stick across the trough, lift a corner of the paper with the hand, and pull it back over the stick: when half of it is placed, take hold of the stick with your right hand and remove the paper completely. Carry it with the stretcher, allowing the mucilage to fall into the drip tray, where it gathers. Check the paper to see if the colors have been well done and that the colors adhere firmly to the paper and leave no grain; if this is not the case, add a little gall. The paper should have small double and triple circles, with a small circle around each circle. If this small circle does not appear, it is because there is not enough oil, but if its presence is not absolutely necessary, it is not necessary to add oil because it would be necessary to start the first operation again, and it is better to leave the pattern a little flat than to repeat the operation because it could result in not sufficiently milling the oil, which would then leave small round spots in the patterns, a circumstance that also occurs when the oil was not sufficiently milled the first time. There is no good solution for this. The only thing that can be tried is to stir the color with the brush so that the small oil spots become even smaller.

The marbler must be careful to adopt the best way to strike with a brush; everything depends on this operation to have the paper evenly colored. He must be able to say, for example, I want to make large, medium or small marbling. Moreover, if you want to have very small marbling, you must put very little color in the brush, and instead of tapping on your hand, tap on a piece of hardwood or even on rounded iron, and repeat the strokes four, five and even six times.

The first day that one is working on freshly prepared mucilage, the work is more difficult, and the bath is too strong; but when one has worked for a day, and when one has put back into the bath, the water that has run off from the sheets, the bath becomes more manageable and milder, and the pattern more consistent. When you have worked for a few hours, and the trough is no longer so full, you must add fresh mucilage mixed with the water that has been drained from the sheets, and you must re-mix it and skim it.

If there are two workers, then there is one who marbles and the other (usually an apprentice) who puts the sheets and removes them.

The papers are placed on the stretcher, one next to the other, but without touching, and when the stretcher is loaded, it is taken by two people and placed on the highest tier. It is left there for some time so that the size that it still retains falls into the drain channel. When it has completely drained off, it is moved back and left to dry. When it is dry, remove it, take it in both hands and smooth it.

These are the most basic marbled papers that are made with several colors simultaneously; we will, therefore, call the preliminary work the *background color* and the colors applied to it, the *vein colors*.

TO PREPARE THE VEIN COLOR, PROCEED AS FOLLOWS: Mix 150–200 grams (5–6 oz.) of paste color in a bowl with glazing paste (with wax and salt of tartar) about the size of a hazelnut. Thin it out with a bit of ox gall, add the color and water, mix thoroughly and strain through a sieve. Avoid using too much water at first because the bowl and sieve can be rinsed, and the wash water adds to the color. Be careful when adding the ox gall, and put in only the amount necessary for the color to spread. The substance should be strong enough to spread out the veins. To make paper with two, three or four veins, the second color must spread the first one, and so on, and finally, the ground must spread them all so that these veins become fine. When making paper with multiple veins, you must not squeeze the veins too tightly or overload them with color because then the colors will run. It is impossible to go into all the practical details of the technique. The marbler must have enough insight to fill in the gaps. If he is diligent, once he has made a few sheets, he can easily see if he has used too much or too little color.

To make the veining, you need a small broom straw brush, and in each bowl, another small bristle brush to stir the color from time to time and pick up the remaining color around the bowl so it doesn't dry. Tap more softly for these kinds of colors. Do not repeat the tapping. Otherwise, the drops will fall on each other too much, especially if there are several veins. (*See specimen № 1.*)[3]

---

3   Specimens begin on page 163.

One can also make a nice marble by using a very lightly speckled background color for the veins and then making the second background with red, blue, green, and yellow, which all must be stronger than the first. One usually chooses a lake color for the yellow veins, but one can always use a little chrome yellow. For the other colors, nothing should be added because if you add another substance, such as white, it would run, and the water would become dirty. It sometimes happens, especially with red lake, that the color curdles and becomes lumpy. It is then advisable to add a few drops of alumina water and a few drops of dissolution of tartaric acid. One operates, moreover, in the same way as for the preceding papers.

N. B. For greater ease, the light colors are speckled first—yellow, red, and blue—and then the black background always being the last.

№ 2. PARTRIDGE EYE   [*Œil de Perdrix*]

The colors are made for the veins and the background in the same way as the previous papers. Only brown is used for the background color. One is free to make the veins as one wishes, but to form the partridge eye, use only red or purple lake.

PREPARATION. In a bowl, take half a kg (1 lb.) of color paste and two spoonfuls of white soap dissolved in water, having the consistency of a good syrup. Add a very small amount of glazing paste, and begin grinding this soap mixture with the thick color, but do not let it foam. When all the color is mixed with the soap, a little water is added, and the mixture is passed through the sieve, after which half a spoonful of potash solution is added, and finally, a little water is added until it is thin enough to be speckled.

Start by speckling the veins, then make the background and finish with the partridge eye, which should form a small round spot that does not spread and does not sink into the mucilage. It should be floating. If it does not float, a little soap should be added; if it spreads, there is too much soap, and a little color and potash should be added. This small dot must be surrounded by a small white circle. If the circle is too small, a little potash should be added, but be careful not to add too much potash; otherwise, the dot will produce rays that are no longer uniform and are not pleasing to the eye.

In the course of the work, it frequently happens that the colors do not want to work anymore, that is to say, that the *spot* does not work well anymore; it is then necessary to add drops of soap or potash.

№ 3. TIGER MARBLE   [*Marbre tigré*]

(*See specimen № 2.*) To make this marble, it is necessary to have old, used mucilage that is mixed with a lot of water; the older this size is, the better the pattern that will be formed, even if this bath is already starting to smell bad.

PREPARATION. The colors for the veins are first prepared as indicated above, and a little German lampblack, known as *Saxon*, is set aside.

This black usually comes in small barrels of 20–25 kg (40–50 lb.). If you don't have any at hand, you can use the black from Landes, but it is not as good. To this black, add a bit of ox gall with a few drops of water and scrub it with the brush; the lampblack will gradually become diluted. Continue until you have prepared enough. If it is too dry, add a little gall. One can also grind this black on a stone with the muller, cut the gall with a little water, and then make it in quite a large amount at the same time because it keeps very well and is even better when it is old than when it is new.

When this color has been well strained, water is added so that it is more or less fluid, like oil and some very strong potash, because the stronger it is, the better. One needs to use *caustic potash* [potassium hydroxide] for this operation and add a little water. When the bath has been beaten, skimmed and left to rest, always cover it with paper (old sheets of stained paper are used to cover the bath, dried after each use, and kept for this purpose). The color is then tested. First, the veins are applied, then the color for the tiger, which must fall in small drops and which, depending on the way it falls, will throw varying rays on all sides. For this pattern, it is necessary to only use a very light broom straw brush. If the falling drops are too large, which sometimes happens when the color is too thick, a little water is added, and if it does not squeeze the veins enough, then the color is not strong, and a little ox gall and potash must be added. When the color is not working properly, i.e., when the rays are no longer properly formed, a few drops of potash should be added. The marble worker must be attentive and observe all these details, and with some care, he will know, in a short time, to recognize all the defects or mishaps that may occur. On the other hand, he must not overload the color with potash; otherwise, the small black drop would burn and become yellow.

It is also necessary to be very careful not to repeatedly come back while speckling; otherwise, the drops will fall one on top of the other, and the pattern will become blurred, but one can make the drops tight.

№ 4. SCHROËTEL MARBLE   [*Marbres Schroëtel*]

Schroëtel is the name they gave this pattern in Germany, and since no other word can be found for it, they have kept the name in France. (*See specimen № 5.*)

To make this marbled paper, one combines three parts of very old psyllium mucilage and one part of gum tragacanth mucilage that has already been used. These two mucilages are mixed well together, and the procedure is the same as for other patterns.

The colors for the veins are prepared in the same way, then a spoonful of the white soap from Marseilles is taken from a bowl and a little, but very little, ox gall is added. Mix with the color, and pour in a little potash (always *red American potash* or *caustic potash*, dissolved in a little water, then decanted) and a few drops of alum.

Cassel brown [Vandyke brown] can also be used, prepared according to the instructions in № 1, and prepared in oil for a final color, but the spotting must not be overdone; otherwise, the color for the background would not have enough strength. To disperse the color, use a straw brush that is neither too coarse nor too fine.

You can hardly use any other color for this marble than the red or purple lake. You can also make green with finely ground indigo, mixed with yellow lake, or blue with indigo alone. Other colors are not suitable for this purpose.

№ 5. LARGE STONE MARBLE   [*Marbres gros cailloux*]

This paper is very nice for large works, either books or paperboards, because the design covers well, and one can create very brilliant veins on it. (*See specimen № 3.*)

The bath is prepared with psyllium seed mucilage, which is not too thin and not too old.

The color for the veins is prepared as usual, and the larger speckles are thrown down.

Cassel brown [Vandyke brown] is finely ground with very strong potash water and placed in a bowl, adding little by little a solution of soap, about 32 grams (1 oz.) of soap for half a kg of brown, and a very small amount of ox gall. The whole is mixed well together, then when the veins have been speckled, the brown color, known as the *background color*, is thrown on to form the stones. It is necessary that the drops are about the size of a large pea and spread out to the diameter of a walnut. If one tests and sees that the color does not spread sufficiently and that it leaves only a small drip on the surface of the water, one adds a little soap dissolved in the water; on the other hand, if it spreads too much, one must add brown and potash. The brush must not be too dense; otherwise, the drops will be too fine. Only Cassel brown can be used.

№ 6. BROKEN MARBLE   [*Marbres cassés*]

To make this marble, you need two tubs that are filled with gum tragacanth mucilage. The bath must be the thickness of a light syrup after having been passed through a sieve into the tub. It is beaten and left to rest, always covered with paper. (*See specimen № 4.*)

The colors for the veins are prepared as before. For the background, the earth colors (Italian yellow, Cassel earth, Italian yellow with indigo for green, or indigo by itself for blue) are ground with ox gall, water, and glazing paste (with wax and salt of tartar). A bit of gall and a hazelnut-sized dollop of glazing paste are enough for half a kg of paste color. A spoonful of lye soap should also be added. It is not possible to specify the exact quantity of gall that should be used because some galls have more strength than others; this quantity also depends on the bath. The older and thinner the bath, the more the color will spread, but it is not advisable to make a bath too thin because the color will not stay stable, and the pattern will not be well-formed. The marble maker must be attentive and apply all his skills to this work.

As always, speckle, the veins first, then the background that is to break up, leaving the tub uncovered. Repeat the same operation on the second tub. While speckling the color on the second tub, the color is working (breaking up) in the first. There should always be a second tub, so the colors have time breaks up in the interval. To obtain this breakdown, it is necessary to be very careful to put enough gall and soap to produce this effect; if it does not break enough, that is to say, if the pattern (of the background) comes too smooth, then there is too much gall, and it is necessary to add color and soap. On the contrary, if it breaks too much, add a little color but no gall until it has been tested.

A very nice paper is made when, after having speckled the veins, take a feather or a small stick and draw lines along the length of the bath, going back and forth in the bath, then the color becomes a thousand stripes, after which speckle the background, which spreads it out and squeezes it. The whole thing produces a very nice effect. An important instruction is to gently put the paper on the gum base because each movement will leave a mark.

№ 7. POLISH PAPERS [*Papiers polonais*]
This is a fancy marbled pattern, which has been given this name, and is very elegant, especially when a shaded background (trocadero) is used, as described previously. (*See specimens № 7 and № 8.*)

A. Simple Patterns
The colors for the veins are prepared in three to four shades, for example, yellow, red, blue, and black, and speckled. When this speckling is finished, you draw in the bath, across the trough with a feather or a stick, going back and forth along the length of the bath, then the streaks form a thousand lines, or, instead of drawing lengthwise, you

make small circles that will shape the design. The paper is prepared and taken in hand to be laid down, but instead of laying it down smoothly, small movements are made with the hand, i.e., the paper is pulled back and forth, and the more the movements back and forth are multiplied, the tighter the marks. It is necessary to try to make the marks straight or across the paper, either along its length or from point to point. The paper is laid down with the left hand in the trough, and the other corner is grasped with the right hand, then pulled with the left hand at the same time as the paper is laid down. You must avoid making the marks several times in the same place, and each time you remove the paper you must skim the bath so that it does not become soiled. You can vary the patterns endlessly, changing the graining or the color of the paper and the movements.

B. More Complex Patterns

One operates as before. The colors of the veins are thrown on, drawn out, and then speckled with color prepared as it was for the № 4 Schroëtel pattern. These colors are speckled in very fine drops and left to spread. You can work on two troughs, but you must be very skillful and very fast; otherwise, the cracking will be too intense. When the color is sufficiently cracked, pull through the dots down the length with a 5–6 mm wide comb. Finally, lay the paper on the bath either smoothly or with movement. To save time, you can also draw the veins with a comb, but the dots should be 3–4 cm apart, and it is nice to go back and forth.

№ 8. CHAMPION MARBLE   [*Marbres champions*]

The colors for veins and bath are prepared as above, and for the background, lampblack is ground with ox gall, soap and a little glazing paste. A little potash and alum water are added when the color is ready. When the color has been speckled, it is drawn with a wide comb and the black is speckled after being made to foam, but you must be careful not to make too much foam and speckle with too large drops; otherwise, the *champions* would be too large. By spreading out strongly, the drops form the *champions*. After making this paper, the bath should be left to rest, and the color should be removed because otherwise, the size would become too contaminated. (*See specimen № 6.*)

ENGLISH MARBLES
№ 1. ORDINARY ENGLISH MARBLE
[*Marbres anglais ordinaires*]

This paper is simple and easy to make; it is made on gum tragacanth mucilage. Veins and background are ground with ox gall and glazing paste; the background, or main color, must not be duplicated. While speckling, the drops must fall together and push out the veins in thin lines. (*See specimen № 9.*)

The paper is placed on the bath using a forward and backward motion with the hand so that the pattern becomes shaded. The regularity and width of the shading depend on the marbler: if he wants the shading repeat to be fine, he moves forward and backward quickly, and if he wants the stripes to be wider, he moves forward a little more and less quickly. Every movement of the hand is clearly shown on the paper.

№ 2. COMBED PAPER   [*Papier peignes*]

For this paper, it is necessary to be careful that the bath of gum tragacanth is well prepared. It must not be thicker than a good oil; when one drags it with one's finger, the color should not move; it should not be too thick; otherwise, the colors will not spread on the mucilage. The colors are prepared with ox gall and glazing paste (with wax and salt of tartar), a little potash water and some tartaric acid are added, and a little ox gall diluted with water is put into a bowl. (*See specimen № 10.*)

Three, four or five colors are speckled on the bath, along with tiny drops of water mixed with ox gall. They are drawn through with a pointed stick or a copper wire. To work faster, use a comb measuring 1–2 dm (4–8 in.) in length. This comb shall have teeth of pointed copper wire—each 5–6 cm long—spaced 1–2 cm apart. With this comb, start at the top of the trough, pulling the color very gently toward the bottom. Now drag a width of 1–2 dm (4–8 in.), then bring this pulled color to the edge, pull it to the opposite side, and so on to the other edge of the trough. The comb can be made with a length equal to $1/8$ of the length of the trough, so pulling can be completed in 8 rounds. The whole surface of the trough is then filled with narrow stripes. Take a tightly-toothed comb and insert it into the stripes. Pull it gently from the top of the trough to the bottom, and take care not to push the comb more than one millimeter below the surface of the bath. As soon as you see that the colors are accumulating around the comb's teeth, stop and start again; that is to say, start again from the place where you stopped. When you have finished pulling, lay the paper down gently and then lift it up. The bath must be skimmed between sheets to remove the color that remains on the bath. It is also necessary to use paper that is not excessively sized because the colors will not adhere well. One must have several combs with tight teeth and others with teeth less close together; the tighter the teeth, the smaller and finer the pattern.

To make the combs, take 4 cm (2 in.) wide wooden slats and the length of the trough 3 mm thick. Take hard copper wire 1 mm thick and 12–15 cm (4½–5½ in.) long. Bend the two ends together like a hairpin and nail to one of the slats. Space them evenly depending on the space you want to have between the teeth. Cover it with the other slat and nail it all together to give more stability. Finally, wrap it with twine between the teeth to keep them spaced correctly. Add a small handle in the middle to grasp while pulling and help maintain the comb in balance.

In the same way, various kinds of patterns, antique marbles, or feather marbles can be made. After having speckled the colors, draw with the wide-toothed comb in various patterns such as circles or other shapes.

№ 3. MARBLING ON BOOK EDGES

The marbled book edges are made in the same patterns as those previously described and with the same colors, but it is necessary to use gum tragacanth mucilage size, as the psyllium seed size does not remain calm enough. After the colors have been speckled and the pattern has been made, take books of the same size and grasp them tightly. Gently dip them below the surface of the colors, then shake off the excess size and set them aside. Touch the area of the trough where the colors have been used with a piece of feather soaked in ox gall diluted with water. This water charged with gall must be strong enough so that when one makes a hole in the colors, these will spread out. Now, take the books and dip them on another edge. When all the pattern is used up, the remaining color is skimmed to the front of the trough with a small board, where it is forced to the edge and discarded.

FRENCH MARBLED PAPER

This well-known and highly regarded paper is of great use because of its quality, variety, and vivid colors. It was invented by Mr. F. M. Montgolfier of Annonay and sold under the name of *Annonay paper*. There are three different designs, which are known as *criss-cross* [*croisé*], *trickle* [*coulé*], and spinner [*tourniquet*]. The shades can be varied infinitely by changing the paper from white to colored or using several colors.

The main colors are red, purple, blue, green, and black for the background, and yellow, green, blue, or red for the speckled.

To make the colors, proceed as follows:

Red. Put on the fire in a tinned copper pot 3, 4, or 5 buckets of river water, and for each bucket of water, 500 grams (1 lb.) of pernambuco wood (chopped) and 90 grams (3 oz.) of alum; let it boil for 15–20 minutes, strain it, and put it aside for use. The wood can be boiled a second time, but it will produce a faint color; this second decoction is good for mixing with the first when the color is seen to be too strong.

Violet. In a vat, boil ½ kg (1 lb.) of campêche wood in water and add 100 grams (3 oz.) of alum; after boiling for half an hour, it is drawn off and kept for use.

Blue. Prussian blue in paste is used.

Green. Boil either 250 grams (8 oz.) of Avignon berries or 500 grams (1 lb.) of Persian seed in a pail of water, with 60 grams (2 oz.) of alum for 1–1½ hours, and strain to store. The remnants of the seed may be boiled a second time, and Prussian blue paste is added according to the shade of green desired.

HOW TO MAKE FANCY PAPERS

Black. Take half a kg (1 lb.) of good gallnuts (good gallnuts are small, heavy, and not pitted by worms), 1 kg (2 lb.) of brazilwood, and ½ kg (1 lb.) of copperas, 125 grams (4 oz.) of verdigris, and boil it for 2–3 hours in 3 buckets of water. Remove from the fire and let stand, then strain it through a sieve and boil the residue a second time.

Yellow. Take half a kg (1 lb.) of annatto in a bucket of water or 1 kg (2 lb.) of turmeric powder in a bucket of water with 125 grams (4 oz.) of alum.

To prepare the colors for marbling, take the quantity that you intend to use and put it on the fire. Pour it into a tub or a large bowl with starch, the amount of which varies depending on the volume of color that you want to make. This starch is mixed with the color, and when the color boils, it is poured over the starch, beginning very slowly and then faster, constantly stirring carefully with a wooden spatula until it has the right thickness. Continually stir so that the starch does not clump. Keep some liquid to thin it out in case the colors become too thick. Finally, add some glazing paste. These colors must be fluid enough to easily drop from the brush and run freely. The starch for the blue must be made with water only, and the necessary blue paste is added.

For green, prepare the starch with yellow seed lake and add blue as appropriate for the shade you want. Both annatto and turmeric are good colors for speckling. It can be preserved as a solution. When you want to use the color, thicken it with paste glue and add some glazing paste.

A table of 2½–3 m (8½–9 ft.) in length, 80 cm to 1 m (2½–3 ft.) in width, and 80 cm (2½ ft.) high is used. This table is surrounded by a frame 12–15 cm (5–6 in.) high at the front and angled on both sides. At the front edge, the side panel is 12–15 cm (5–6 in.) high. It increases to 30–36 cm (12–15 in.) at the back. Across the middle of this table, there must be a crossbar going from one end of the table to the other along its length. This bar rests on both sides and is used to put a wood plank in an inclined position so that the color will run easily. This bar must be removable so that it can be taken away when you want to make papers that must be laid flat. The table must rest on four or six legs. One leg on one of the front corners must be a little shorter because a lot of color is thrown on the table. The shorter leg will allow the color to flow to the lowest corner and drain through an opening into a container placed under the table.

It is necessary to have three large wood boards because this paper is usually made in this size. If you want to make other sizes, be sure to have boards the same size as those papers. The boards are placed on the middle bar, with the corners at the bottom and top and slightly angled on the front. Place a bowl for the background color between the boards, and next to that, the color for the speckle. Position them so that the background color will not drip and contaminate the colors.

In front of this table is another small table to put the papers and a small bowl that contains water to sprinkle.

It is necessary to have a turntable, which consists of a square of wood 1–1.3 m (3–4 ft.) high, 10 cm (4 in.) thick, placed on a flat base in a cross; the top of this square piece is cut at an angle, and a square board is attached to it, of such a size that a board can be rested on it; to prevent this board from falling off, the board is surrounded with a small rim half its height or the thickness of the board, so that it can easily be put down and taken up.

One needs a large broom straw brush, a piece of sorbus [ash] wood to strike it against, a sponge to wet the papers, and rods to lie across the stretcher.

White potash (*pearl ash*), for example, half a kg (1 lb.), is dissolved in a liter of hot water, left to stand, drawn out, and preserved.

The alum colors and potash water for watering or wetting should give a slight sediment, and in case they are not effective enough, the quantity of alum or potash should be increased, but always in moderation.

№ 1. CRISS-CROSS [*Papier croisé*][4]

To make this marble, lay the paper on the small table. Use a broom straw brush with potash water. Sprinkle the first sheet and lay it diagonally on a wooden board, with one corner at the bottom and the other at the top.

4 Examples of many of these patterns can be found in the University of Washington Libraries Decorated and Decorative Paper Collection. https://content.lib.washington.edu/dpweb/patterns.html. See "Papier Croisé."

HOW TO MAKE FANCY PAPERS

Use another brush loaded with the color to speckle the dots. Speckle with the background color that is in the bowl on the table between the boards. The speckling is done by striking the broom straw brush against a piece of sorbus [ash] wood until there is enough color on the sheet. This sheet is left, a second one is started, and then a third. When the *third* sheet is done, throw the *first* sheet over a rod with the two points of the paper going in the opposite direction, and lay the color in an **X**. If the color does not flow enough to make the **X**, change to working with two sheets at a time instead of three. Put it on a stretcher to dry. (*See specimen № 12.*)

№ 2. TRICKLE   [*Papier coulé*]

Instead of sprinkling the paper with the brush, it is evenly wetted with potash water using a sponge. The speckle is thrown on, and the paper is placed smoothly on the wood plank; then the background color is speckled, and after making the three sheets, the two corners of the sheet are thrown over a round stick without changing the position so that the color flows and makes straight stripes, and then it is placed on the stretcher. (*See specimen № 11.*)

№ 3. SPINNER
[*Papier tourniquet*]

For the tourniquet paper, remove the bar from the table. Use a flat wooden board beneath the paper, and dampen the sheet with potash water. Wet it so that no excess water remains anywhere that could make hollows. Speckle the sheet, and when it is sufficiently covered, place it—along with the board—on the turntable and spin it in circles until the design is formed. Place another board and sheet on the table and begin again. Do a third sheet, and when this is done, the first should be sufficiently dried to put on a stretcher and carried to the line to dry. (*See specimen № 13.*)

As these papers are generally used for more serious works, do not use fanciful colors; do not use speckles other than yellow, red or blue; for the background, use purple, black, or red, with speckling according to the taste connoisseurs. White or colored papers are used for this production.

This type of paper is also made in Germany, but always with a black ground that combines lampblack prepared with starch and various flecks—two to four colors on the same sheet—which produces a rather pleasant effect. This paper is left to flow across the sheet in a straight line, and when we make papers in shaded colors (trocadero), there are ten to twelve colors on each sheet.

№ 4. AGATE PAPERS
[*Papiers agathes*]

To make agate paper, it is necessary to have 15–20 boards large enough for the paper, several broom straw brushes, bowls, sieves, small brushes for stirring the colors, two small tables, and additional boards to lay the sheets of paper on. (*See specimen № 16.*)

Earth colors must be ground very finely. The usual method is to use silver white, which is a lead white and comes from Klagenfurth in Germany or from Kremnitz in Austria. It comes in small bundles wrapped in blue paper; it is very heavy and difficult to grind; it is sold for 80–90 centimes per half kg (1 lb.). It is imitated in Lille and Clichy, but the quality is not as good. It should not be bought pre-ground from color dealers because it is often mixed with ceruse white. To be on the safe side, grind it yourself or have it ground. Cover it with water; it will keep very well without drying out.

Other colors used are Cassel earth, pale chrome yellow, red lake, yellow lake, violet lake, lampblack, Prussian blue and Berlin blue, golden bronze color—a medium size, not too fine, and Milori green. All these colors need to be ground very fine.

The paper must be strong and well-blended. White paper is primarily used, but colored paper is used for agate, lapis lazuli, emerald and carnelian. In addition, the paper must be well-sized.

High-quality starch is prepared by dissolving it in a large vessel with cold water and pouring boiling water over it until it is transparent; glazing paste made with wax and soap is added, and it is left to cool.

Take about half a kg (1 lb.) of color paste, about the same amount of cooked starch in a perfectly equal and homogeneous way, mix them and pass them through a sieve into the bowl. If the mixture is not thin enough, water is added.

Take a little cooked starch in a bowl, and add water to make it fluid, about one liter of water for 200 grams (7 oz.) of cooked starch, and mix in 10 grams (.4 oz.) of tartaric acid dissolved in water.

The colors for the different agates are prepared as follows:

№ 1. *Sainte-Anne marble*. Grind lampblack with brandy and water, or ox gall and water, and take a decoction of gallnut, with vitriol and a part of purple lake; mix with cooked starch, about as much starch as color, and mix in a little glazing paste.

Lampblack by itself is also ground previously described, mixed with starch and some glazing paste, but not too much.

Silver white ground with about twice its weight of starch and very little glazing paste.

A sheet of white paper is dampened with water prepared with starch and tartaric acid using a soft brush. Pass over the sheet lengthwise and widthwise so that it is well and evenly dampened. Carry on a board that must be laid flat on a table. Pure lampblack is speckled on with a broom straw brush in small drops over the whole of its surface, but not too densely. Speckle the black mixed with gallnut and purple lake in much larger drops, again, not too densely. Finally, load a brush with white and speckle it quite densely with small drops. Take the sheet of speckled paper at both corners, on the width of the board, and hold it with two fingers, thumb and forefinger, on this board so that it can not fall; tip the board with the paper perpendicularly and knock it two, three, or more times so that the color will flow down. Each drop must move down 30–40 mm. Turn the board on the opposite side and give a few more knocks to make the color flow down in the other direction, but very little this time. You can also give it a few more knocks on the other side to help form the design, especially the white color, which must make zigzags to form the veins of the agate or marble. If the color ran too much, then the sheet was too wet, or the color was too liquid. If it did not flow, then the paper was not wet enough, or the color was too thick. Leave the sheet on the board and wait until it is dry enough to put on the drying line.

№ 2. *Lapis-lazuli*. White or light blue dyed paper:

Berlin blue ⎫ always mixed with
Prussian blue ⎰ starch and glazing paste

Silver white

Powdered bronze with a little starch but no glazing paste; otherwise, it would quickly turn black

The bronze should be speckled in small drops that spread out. The bronze should not be ground but instead well-mixed.

№ 3. *Emerald*. The paper is lightly tinted green with a little azure. The paper is usually dyed green but very lightly (all dyed papers must be made in rolls so that the colors will flow well).

Milori green—small drops.

Green made from yellow lake and Prussian blue—large drops.

Prussian blue—small drops.

Silver white—small and medium drops, very close together.

№ 4. *Carnelian*. White paper

Red lake—small tight drops

Red lake mixed with yellow lake—large drops, more fluid color

Red lake, purple lake, yellow lake, and a little Cassel earth—small tight drops

Cassel earth with a little black—small drops

Silver white—medium drops, not too tightly spaced

№ 5. *Egyptian*

Black—small drops

Cassel earth—small drops

Yellow lake mixed with a little Cassel earth—medium drops

Silver white—small and tight drops

HOW TO MAKE FANCY PAPERS

№ 6. *Brown*

      Cassel earth—large drops

      Yellow lake—medium drops

      Purple lake—small drops

      Red lake—small drops

      Silver white—medium and tight drops

№ 7. *Green*

      Green № 1

      Pale chrysanthemum yellow—medium drops

      Milori green—medium drops

      Silver white—medium and small tight drops

      Green № 2

      Pale chrome yellow—small tight drops

      Yellow lake—medium-sized drops spaced out

      Milori green—medium-sized drops

      Berlin blue—small tight drops

      Silver white—small and medium tight drops

№ 8. *White Marble*

      Lampblack, gallnut and violet lake, very fluid and small drops scattered

      Berlin blue, very small drops and spaced out

      Silver white, medium drops and tightly spaced

      Very small drops of brown—made with yellow, red and purple lakes—
can be added, but they must be widely spaced out.

Many agates and marbles of the imagination can be made this way
to imitate any natural marbles. It is only necessary that the manufacturer has vision and intelligence. One can gather the colors that drip
down from speckling and use them for browns or grays.

One must always operate as indicated for pattern № 1 and leave
the sheet of paper laid flat until it is dry enough so that the color no
longer runs.

In all the colors, it is necessary to add glazing paste (soap and wax),
but use very little; otherwise, they will not come glossy when polished.

№ 5. ROOT PAPERS   [*Papiers racines*]

This paper is of great use for bookbinding, and very fine ones can be made, but great care must be taken. (*See specimen № 17.*)

For this purpose, use manila paper, well glued, and give it a layer of color.

Tan. Yellow ochre paste with paste glue and glazing paste.

A more beautiful tan. Italian yellow in paste and glazing paste.

Yellow. Yellow lake and glazing paste.

Golden apple. Orange lead, strongly ground with water and glazing paste.

Red. Red lake.

White. Silver white, strongly glued, and glazing paste. It is ground and compressed so that it is uniform.

It is necessary to have two large tubs. One usually uses a 300-liter barrel and cuts it in half.

Two trestles are made in the shape of a St. Andrew's cross (an **X**) and are placed 1–1 ½ m apart (3–4 ½ ft.). The upper **V**, or top, is lined with boards. The device is sloped so the water can easily run off; it is a good idea to have it sealed with tar on the inside, especially the joints so water does not run through; it is called a *channel* or a *gutter*. At the top, it must have an opening of 60–65 cm (22–24 in.). Two bars are attached to this opening, and a square board is placed upon them, leaving a space of 65 cm (2 ft.) on the left side of the gutter. Strong nails are driven into this board every 3–4 cm (1–1 ½ in.). Between these nails, small round or pointed pebbles are stuffed along the whole length of the board, so they leave gaps so that when a sheet of paper is placed on them, there will be unevenness—cavities or low parts. At the end of this channel, place one of the tubs that have been filled with water. The rinse water should flow into this tub. A frame to spread the paper across for washing is also nailed across this tub. On the left side of the board with the pebbles, arrange a small tub filled with about 1–2 bucketfuls of water and a large wooden spoon.

Another tub is placed in front of the channel, about 65 cm (2 ft.) away. A round stick is attached in the middle (across the width) and placed so that the opening slopes toward the back, and the surface forms a cone. There is no need to use too much liquid because it will collect at the front.

On the right side of the pebble board is a large stoneware bowl.

In a corner, close to the rooter [worker], place a small table measuring 65 cm (2 ft.) square to put the paper.

To prepare, dissolve copperas in a stoneware pot and add gallnuts from Aleppo—the most beautiful are always the cheapest. Crush everything and boil it in a copper boiler using about four liters of river water to half a kg (1 lb.) of gallnut. Boil until the gallnut is quite soft. Strain and store it for use. It is good not to overcook at first because the decoction will soon become moldy and lose its characteristics.

Throw a few kg of true red American potash in a stoneware pot, cover it with water and let it stand.

It is necessary to have a long, soft square brush, a large, tight broom straw brush, and a small broom about one-third the size of an ordinary broom. The broom straw brush should be soaked in water for 24 hours. The loose pieces should fall out when it is wrung out well. A round iron bar of 18–20 mm in diameter and 45 cm (18 in.) long to knock against, a few earthen pots, and 4–5 round poles about 65 cm (2 ft.) long. The broom straw brush is placed on the stoneware bowl on the right side, and a broom in a small bucket filled with water is placed on the left side so that the rooter has all his utensils within reach. A clay pot should be hung in the tub in front of the gutter.

All being thus arranged, one is prepared then to root. Put the paper on the small table beside the bowl with the gallnut decoction. Pour dissolved copperas into the large stoneware bowl and water into the small tub next to it, and then fill one of the large tubs with water. Pour a prepared dissolution of potash into the other large tub. This dissolution of potash doesn't need to be too strong; one tries it by tasting it. It must sting enough but not burn. The solution of copperas must be transparent and free from impurities.

Four to five round sticks are attached to the side of the table to be made so that the paper can be laid over each stick separately.

Take the gallnut decoction and brush it on a sheet of paper lengthwise and widthwise so it is well-saturated. Place this sheet on a stick, prepare another the same way, and continue until you have done four.

When this is done, the first sheet is taken up again and placed on the round bar attached to the potash tub so that the sheet lies in the middle. Potash water is poured over it with the earthen jug that is hanging inside the tub for this purpose. It is necessary to be very careful to pour well evenly and to make sure that the potash water flows nicely over the entire sheet. It is necessary to pour twice so the potash water should not be too strong. When this is done, replace the sheet that has been treated with the potash with another, and in the interval of this second operation, the sheet in the tub should be dry enough to be removed. It is then placed on the pebble board, and another sheet is put in its place. There must always be three sheets on the rods, one sheet in the potash, and one sheet on the pebbles. The rooter then takes the copperas with his broom straw brush, and after thoroughly wiping his brush, he passes it with the iron bar from the right hand into the left hand; then, with the right hand, he takes the broom, which is on the water in the small tub, and sprinkles the sheet on the pebbles, and immediately puts the brush back in place, and begins to speckle with the copperas water—the smaller the drops, the better the results. The brush must be raised so that the tip is in the air and knocked quickly and evenly. The water that has been sprinkled flows over the sheet into the crevices and causes the copperas to swirl and form the roots. The sheet is left for some time in this state, and in the meantime, another sheet is started with the gall. When the roots are dark enough, take a big spoonful of water from the large tub, pour it over the sheet and put it on the screen above the water tub. Pour more water over it and rinse it well so there is no copperas left but the roots, and repeat the same operation.

Start with four sheets, but if the first sheet is not sufficiently dried, work with five. If the sheets become too dry, which happens in hot weather, only three are used, and if the copperas does not want to settle properly, it is because the potash water is too strong or the decoction of gallnut is too weak. The roots all appear grey if the gallnut is not strong enough—particularly when the potash is weak.

The gallnut must be absorbed into the sheet but not be allowed to dry out.

Usually, three to four handfuls of paper can be placed on the large tub, the sheets one on top of the other; commonly, three to four hours of work, and they are moved to the lines to dry, but they must be well washed because if copperas water remains, there will be black places. In general, it is advisable not to spare the water.

The roots described will come out black, but if you want to make blue or speckled roots, use a solution of prussiate of potash and copperas water, each separately, and pour a solution of tartaric acid into the water in the large tub. (Diluted nitric acid could also be used, but it might burn the paper).

In this manner, the root is made blue, and if you use canary yellow paper, the root will become green. If one wants blue, brown, and red roots on the same sheet, make a decoction of pernambuco wood in copperas water; no alum would be needed in the decoction. Speckle well with prussiate of potash, and apply red copperas afterward to obtain three shades of roots.

A much more beautiful and pronounced root is obtained if the paper is sized once or even twice with strong glue before it is rooted.

To make root paper for smaller book formats, construct frames with compartments of the desired size. Place them on the pebble board so that the hollows and projections form the root in a very uniform way.

§ V. Monochromatic Papers

Plain-colored papers are very easy to make. All that is needed to succeed is to become accustomed to handling the brush: for this purpose, use soft bristle brushes, 12–15 cm (5–6 in.) long, 4–5 cm wide, round brushes of hog's bristle, very long, and a bowl measuring 30–40 cm (12–15 in.) in diameter. (*See specimen № 18.*)

The worker must load the brush with as much color as he deems necessary to color the entire sheet in one go and brush the sheet briskly enough and in both directions so as not to leave any streaks. Once the paper is covered, the color is smoothed out using the brush, always working in circles. Grasp the handle of the brush and move the tip of the bristles over the paper until it is uniformly tinted.

Choose paper that is well and evenly sized, has no bumps, and is flat and not creased.

Any paper to which a second coat is to be applied must be perfectly dry before it is pressed. It must be pressed evenly and firmly; otherwise, the second layer will not come out well.

Glazing paste made from wax and flour (№ 1) is added to each color. When the color is prepared, a sheet is made, dried, and polished to see if there is enough glazing paste and if the desired shade has been achieved.

One usually prepares color only for the day because the remaining will spoil, especially in the heat; if this happens, it must be used immediately.

Usually, two people are involved in this operation—a workman and an apprentice who acts as the spreader.

The spreader/apprentice must be skilled enough that just as the workman has finished a sheet, he grabs it, removes it, and places it on the holder to lay it on the lines. He places the sheet on his holder so that it is two-thirds on one side and one-third on the other so he can more easily place it across the ropes from the middle.

A wooden spoon is usually left in the color for the apprentice to occasionally stir the color, especially the heaviest ones.

The workers sometimes place two reams of paper on the table, but this way of working is not the best because, in the heat, the edges of the paper will dry and stick together.

The workman holds the paper with his left hand and does not press too much with the brush to keep the paper from sliding.

Never let the brush and the brush loaded with color dry, but always wash them as soon as you finish working.

The color should not be too thick. It should have the consistency of a good syrup. The exact quantity of color required cannot be specified. It depends on the shade—lighter or darker—that you want to achieve and the color. Certain colors cover better than others depending on the nature and the kind of color used.

To make them beautiful, high-quality dark papers, you need to use two layers of color. One could make them dark with only one layer, but the colors are never as equal and beautiful.

The color and the paste glue are added to a large bowl and ground together. When this is done, a sieve large enough to cover the second bowl is placed on two rounded wooden bars, and the color is passed through the sieve into the second bowl and thinned with the wash water from the brush and the bowl.

For the paper with two coats, the color bath does not need to be as strong for the second coat as for the first.

When the paper is dry, it is smoothed, and the folds are removed by hand. Usually, it is burnished with a flat stone polishing machine. There are sometimes colors that do not want to go to the polishing machine. In this case, make a ball with woolen rags, rub it with yellow wax, and run it over the paper. One can also use very fine powdered talc and rub the paper with it. To increase the quality, use a light bath of starch prepared with boiling water and glazing paste (soap and wax). One can easily polish the sheet and obtain a superb gloss. Putting too much glazing paste is unnecessary, and the bath needs to be very thin.

PREPARATION OF COLORS FOR
THE MONOCHROMATIC PAPERS
Based on about one ream of large-sized paper.

№ 1. Morocco Red

1st coat

Orange lead	2	kg
Paste glue	3	—

2nd coat

Red lake, depending on how dark you want it to be	1½—2	kg
Paste glue	2½	—

№ 2. Dark Red

Dark red lake 3   kg

Paste glue 4   —

To make it very dark, use the remaining color to make a second coat when you have finished the ream.

№ 3. Medium Red

Dark red lake 2   kg

Paste glue 4   —

№ 4. Pink

Dark red lake 1   kg

Spanish white dissolved in water . . . . 1½   —

Paste glue 4   —

To make it lighter, use less dark red or more Spanish white. Zinc white, which is common and inexpensive, can also be used. With this type of white, the shades are more beautiful.

№ 5. Dark Blue

Prussian blue paste 3   kg

Paste glue 4   —

№ 6. Medium Blue

Prussian blue paste 2   kg

Paste glue 4   —

№ 7. Light Blue

Prussian blue paste	1½	kg
Zinc white	1	—
Paste glue	4	—

Do not use Spanish or Meudon white for the white. It will turn gray.

№ 8. Fine Blue

Fine blue paste	4	kg
Paste glue	4	—

The color will be a little strong.

№ 9. Dark Green

Yellow lake	1½	kg
Prussian blue paste	2	—
Paste glue	4½	—

Layer two coats of the same color so they are both beautiful and dark.

№ 10. Medium Green

Use the same proportions and apply only one layer.

№ 11. Light Green

Prussian blue paste	1	kg
Yellow lake	1	—
Zinc white	1	—
Paste glue	4	—

The formula depends on the shade you want to obtain. For a bluish color, add more blue; otherwise, add more yellow lake.

№ 12. Fine Green

Make a first layer with

Prussian blue paste 1	kg
Yellow lake 1	—
Zinc white 1	—
Paste glue 4	—

And a second layer with:

Schweinfurt green paste 3	kg
Watery paste glue 3	—

Twelve liters of water are used as a basis for the watery glue and mixed with one kg of strong, first-quality glue. For a richer color, apply two coats, keep the color solution stronger, and apply glazing paste № 2 (wax and soap).

№ 13. Yellow

1½ kg turmeric in powder is boiled with ¼ kg alum dissolved in 12 liters of water. It is mixed with water and left to cool. If you want to use it, take some paste glue and mix it with this decoction, depending on the shades you want to obtain.

№ 14. Second Yellow

Yellow lake 2	kg
Paste glue 3	—

№ 15. Third Yellow

Yellow chrome paste 2	kg
Paste glue 3	—

№ 16. Golden Apple Yellow

Dark chrome yellow 1   kg
Orange lead powder 1   —
Paste glue 4   —

№ 17. Orange

Orange lead powder 3   kg
Paste glue, and hold the bath stronger 4   —

№ 18. Tan

Yellow Italian earth 2   kg
Paste glue 4   —

№ 19. Violet

Violet lake . . . . 1½   kg
Paste glue 3   —

№ 20. Lilac

Red lake 1   kg
Violet lake . . . . ½   —
Prussian blue paste . . . . ½   —
Zinc white 2   —
Paste glue 3   —

To give the lilac a blue tint, use more Prussian blue; to make it pink-ish, use more red.

№ 21. Black

Lampblack soaked in brandy;		
or ox gall mixed with water	½	kg
Hide glue.	2½	—

№ 22. Gray

Lampblack	⅛	kg
Meudon white or zinc white	2	—
Paste glue	3	—

№ 23. Brown

Italian red crushed in water	1	kg
Lampblack	¼	—
Yellow lake	½	—
Paste glue	3	—

Several variations of brown can be made by using more or less of the yellow and black or adding either Meudon white or zinc white.

§ VI. Quilted, Jaspered or Marloborough Papers
[Papiers Piqués, Jaspés Ou Marloborough]

The colors are prepared in the same way as for the plain papers, but the bath is made a bit stronger, and the sheet is more heavily colored. (*See specimens 19 and 20.*)

For *piqué* [quilted] paper, put a little color on the table and rub the tip of the brush with it so that it takes on some moisture. Then, the paper is colored by brushing over it lengthwise and widthwise. The color is likewise tapped with the tip of the brush to make what is called the *piqué*.

For *jasper* paper, load the sheet with color using a brush as before. Take a sponge that has been loaded with color from the table and tap the sheet. This is the way to make the jasper paper. For a larger mottled pattern, use more color on the sheet; for a smaller pattern, use less.

It is necessary to choose a well-rounded sponge, not too golden, with equal-sized hollows or pores, to wash it with weak hydrochloric acid and to remove the concretions and the sand it may contain.

For *Marlborough* paper, one sheet of paper is colored and set aside. A second sheet is colored and immediately covered with the first. To do this, the worker takes the first sheet by two corners and lays this second sheet precisely on the first one, with colored sides together. Take a brush and tap the sheets with the tip. When the sheets are placed one on top of the other, they sometimes trap air bubbles. These should be avoided or removed because if they are too big, they will cause unevenness in the jasper pattern. Separate the two sheets to hang them on the lines to dry.

§ VII. Wood Grain Papers [*Papier bois*]

Wood grain papers are made with yellow Italian earth paste, sometimes mixed with orange lead, chrome yellow, a little black, or Cassel earth, depending on the desired shade. The colors are mixed with paste glue and glazing paste. (*See specimen № 21.*)

The sheet of paper is colored a little heavily but evenly with a stiff brush. The brush is dragged either lengthwise or widthwise, sometimes giving a slight wavy movement with the hand so as not to make straight lines. This creates the lines or grain. In some places, burrs or knots are formed by twisting the tip of the brush in circles or ovals.

Fine-quality wood grain paper is made using vellum or strong paper. For this, it is necessary to use rabbit hide glue or strong glue instead of paste glue. Use 12 liters of water per half kg (1 lb.) of glue and mix with the colors mentioned before. Make a leather comb. For this, take a piece of hard leather, e.g., thin sole leather, 15–16 cm (5–6 in.) long by 5 cm (2 in.) wide. Even it out well in thickness and make uneven notches like the teeth of a comb; using this tool and making a slight undulating movement with the hand, draw in long, ovoid, tapering, and half-round strokes. In this way, we imitate the roots or grain of the wood. When the paper is dry, it is smoothed, pressed and varnished.

§ VIII. Granite Papers
[*Papiers granit*]

Prepare any color you want, but do not use too much paste glue. It is better to use hide glue and glazing paste (with wax with salt of tartar) and keep the color thin. Little color is needed for an entire ream of paper. Next to the color bowl is a square, plain board on which a little color is thrown. Use a tightly woven brass wire mesh screen with a handle, 30–36 cm (12–14 in.) square and 3–4 cm (1–1½ in.) deep. Cover the screen with color from the board and hold it by the handle 26–28 cm (9–10 in.) above the paper. Rub the color through the screen with a brush to create a cloud or mist of color that will fall very finely on the paper until it is sufficiently filled. (*See specimen № 14.*)

This granite can be made with several colors on the same sheet. For this, it is necessary to use a separate board, brush, and screen for each color. Otherwise, the paper can be made with only one color. After the first color has been put on, the sheet is dried, put in a press, and the process is repeated for the next color.

§ IX. Barley Grain Paper   [*Papier grains d'orge*]

Barley grain paper is made in the same way as granite, but before starting with the color, barley grains are thrown on the sheets in patches and not too evenly. (This pattern is basically granite with blank patches.) This is made by dropping more barley in some places and less in others. The color is applied as it is for the granite paper. When the color is finished, the sheet is turned over so that the grains fall away. All the places that were protected by grains will remain as unfilled patches of the background color.

§ X. Satin-like Papers   [*Papiers satinés*]

The numerous uses and the great consumption of satin-like papers mean that we must concern ourselves seriously with them. There are very few establishments that manufacture this paper well. As a result of competition, ordinary colors are used and applied in a single thick coat so the sheets can be sold at a lower price. To make satin-like papers well, it is necessary to use very good colors and to make two or three coats for certain colors. Use earth or mineral colors, well ground, and apply them carefully and evenly on the paper without leaving brush strokes. Use the same brush and the same brushes as for the solid colors. The colors are more opaque than those for plain paper; because of this, they will show all the finger marks made when touching them. Care must be taken, and when the worker removes the sheet to put it on the lines, it must be held at the very corner and only with the fingertips. (*See specimen № 22.*)

It is necessary to choose a very white paper, naturally, quite plain and well-sized.

For all the colors, use glazing paste with soap and wax. For a ream of paper, use 50–60 grams (1½–2 oz.) of this glue (mixed to the thickness of an ointment), strong Flanders glue, and—even for soft colors—gelatin.

Flanders glue, or gelatin, is melted in river water on a low fire and then allowed to cool. (Flanders glue must be soaked in water for 24 hours before use.) In this state, it will be "shaky," and when it is to be used, it must be heated. When they are done and cooled, the colors gel and must be heated on a very light fire so as not to bring them to a too high temperature, especially for the second coat; otherwise, this coat would destroy the first coat. Before starting this work, make a sheet and let it dry to see if the color has sufficiently adhered and if the paper comes out shiny when rubbed with a glazing brush. Or fold a corner of the paper and rub it. If the color flakes off, there is insufficient glue, and more must be added. If, when rubbing with the brush, it slides too easily, there is too much glazing paste. For the second coat, it is better to begin with very little glazing paste because more can always be added.

A lot of glossy or satin papers are used for lithographic prints. These papers must use very little glue (or even none at all) because the pressure of the cylinder will provide enough shine.

When the paper is completely dry, it must be prepared carefully to avoid creases and placed in pairs, color by color. When the paper is ready, use a round brush of 15–16 cm (5–6 in.) in diameter, very tight, with stiff, short bristles. Brush until the sheet is shiny, then beat it on a marble slab with a gold beater's hammer, taking three to four hands of paper at a time and pounding them equally. (Note: Since every blow produces a mark, we hardly ever beat the paper anymore but instead roll it between zinc plates after it has been brushed.)

This paper becomes very shiny when it is burnished the English way, i.e., twice lengthwise and once widthwise. For those papers that are hard to polish, it is necessary to use a little more glazing paste, especially with the colors green of Schweinfurt and ultramarine. In general, a lot of ceruse white is used. Always make a test or proof sheet before proceeding with the actual work.

PREPARATION OF COLORS FOR
SATIN OR GLOSSY PAPER
Based on about one ream of large-sized paper.

№ 1. Morocco Red

1st coat

Orange lead powder	2	kg
Ceruse white paste	½	—
Hide glue	3	—
Glazing paste	60	gm

2nd coat

Cochineal lake paste	1½	kg
Hide glue	1	—

A little glazing paste

№ 2. Red

Carmine lake	2	kg
Hide glue	1½	—

A little glazing paste

To get a deep color, apply two coats.

№ 3. Pink

Carmine Lake	1	kg
Ceruse white paste	2½	—
Hide glue.	3	—
A little glazing paste		

If a lighter red is desired, then ceruse white is added; for a darker red, more lake would be added. Many beautiful shades can be created by adding white.

№ 4. Dark Blue

1st coat

Prussian blue paste	2	kg
Hide glue.	2½	—
Glazing paste	60	gm

2nd coat

Berlin blue.	1	kg
Hide glue.	1½	—
Glazing paste	60	gm

№ 5. Very Dark Blue

Apply the first coat in black color and the second with Prussian blue.

№ 6. Steel Blue

This can be done in several ways:
- A. The first coat in black.
- B. The first coat in Prussian blue.
- C. The first coat in violet. The second coat with steel white, or two coats with steel blue.

It is not possible to specify the quantity of steel blue color to use for a ream of paper because this color is not always identical: it depends on the shade that one wishes to obtain and whether it is light or dark. It requires a lot of blue to be strongly bonded. Use glazing paste № 1 (wax and flour) because the other glue will change the tone.

№ 7. Light Blue

Berlin blue	1	kg
Ceruse white paste	2½	—
Hide glue	3	—
A little glazing paste		

№ 8. Fine Blue

Fine blue paste	3 to 4	kg
Ceruse white	1½	—
Hide glue	4	—
A little glazing paste		

You can make a fine blue of a rather beautiful tone with these materials:

Prussian blue paste	1½	kg
Granular bismuth white, to be ground	½	—
Hide glue	2½ to 3	—
Glazing paste	60	gm

When the color bath is done, potash water is added with pearl ash until the blue begins to turn grayish, then tartaric acid dissolved in water is poured until the blue returns; the hue will appear faded but more beautiful.

№ 9. Ultramarine

The variations in this color are so great that it is impossible to specify the proportions to be used.

It is necessary to grind this color since it is in powder form. Grind it with water, and for each half kg (1 lb.) of dry color, add 2–2½ kg (4–5 lbs.) of hide glue and 65–100 gm (2–3 oz.) of glazing paste. This paper is difficult to make in two coats. It is made in one coat with a slightly stronger color or with a first coat of Prussian blue and ceruse white.

№ 10. Dark Green

Milori green in granules
which must be ground . . . . ¾ to 1   kg
Ceruse white . . . . 1 to 1½   —
Hide glue 3   —
Glazing paste

This color will cover very well: then it can be done in one layer, or you
can give the second coat with a more watery color.

№ 11. Fine Green

Schweinfurt green paste 3   kg
Ceruse white . . . . 1½   —
Hide glue 4   —
Glazing paste 100   gm

This color doesn't cover well, and you need to apply at least two coats,
or you can do the first coat with Milori green or English green and the
second with Schweinfurt green.

№ 12. Yellow

Chrome yellow paste 2   kg
Ceruse white paste . . . . 2½   —
Hide glue 4   —
Glazing paste 60   gm

№ 13. Tan

Italian yellow paste . . . . 1 to 1½   kg
Ceruse white with water 2   —
Hide glue 4   —
Glazing paste 60   gm

№ 14. Black

Lampblack crushed with ox gall and water or brandy and water.	1	kg
Hide glue.	3–4	—
Glazing paste	60	gm

№ 15 Grey

Ceruse white with water	3	kg
Hide glue.	4	—
Glazing paste	60	gm
Lampblack ground to the desired shade		

№ 16. Orange

Orange lead powder	2 to 2½	kg
Ceruse white paste	1 to 1½	—
Hide glue.	4	—
A little glazing paste		

№ 17. White

Silver white paste	4–5	kg
White hide glue	5–6	—
A little glazing paste		

Many more shades can be made, and it is quite easy for the craftsman to mix them, but you will always need ceruse white and glazing paste.

§ XI. Fire-Glazed Paper
[*Papier lissé au feu*]

This is called *fire-glazed paper* because of its brilliant sheen. The name is particularly appropriate for marbled papers in red, green and blue colors. Because this glossy sheen is obtained by the use of varnish, it can also be used for morocco, securities papers or embossed papers. (*See specimen № 15.*)

PREPARATION

Melt half a kg (1 lb.) of Flanders or Cologne glue (Cologne glue is whiter and stronger) in 6–8 liters of water. When it is well melted, add 250 grams (8 oz.) of alum powder. When the glue becomes very thick, nitric acid is added until the glue becomes as clear, more or less, as it was before the alum was added. It is left to cool, and a very small amount of glazing paste is added. This glue will remain somewhat liquid but keep its strength. This glue will be applied to the paper to varnish it. Apply one or two coats. (It is better to apply these two lighter coats than one heavy coat.) When the paper is dry, it is polished with a very smooth round stone using short strokes to bring out the gloss. This varnish is advantageous, especially for morocco or securities papers, because it can be gilded without glairing. In Germany, this glue is used instead of greasy varnish.

§ XII. Embossed like Morocco Leather or Moiré Fabric
[*Papiers Maroquinés ou gouffrés, moirés chagrinés*]

Follow the same process of preparation of the colors as for the plain papers, but use carmine lake instead of red lake. Apply two layers. Pass the paper through two cylinders, one of which, the top one, is made of copper engraved with, e.g., a design for the morocco, and the other one for the moiré, or engraved with a drawing of flowers or arabesques, and the other one made of paper, to make the counterpart. You need a pair of cylinders for each design. (It is a good idea to contact M. Plain, engraver, rue Aumaire, 42, who engraves almost all the cylinders used in France and even in England.) When the paper has been passed through the cylinders, it is varnished with copal varnish and left to dry for 2–3 days. It can also be varnished before passing through the cylinders, but in this case, it is necessary to operate 6–8 days before; otherwise, the varnish would not be dry enough, and there would be a risk that the paper would remain between the cylinders.

For fire glazing, the paper must be varnished and polished before passing through the cylinders so that it will become beautiful. (*See specimens № 23, № 24, and № 25.*)

§ XIII. Papers for Artificial Flowers

These are fine papers that are dyed on both sides with watercolors. The finest-quality colors are generally used in this production, and several kinds of these papers are made for the flowers, the leaves, and the rest.

Red. For red flowers, cochineal is crushed and boiled in a well-tinned pot. Take half a kg (1 lb.) of cochineal, 90–100 grams (3–4 oz.) of cream of tartar, and 32 grams (1 oz.) of volatile alkali and boil. (The residue is boiled a second time and used for pink papers or lighter reds.)

Once the color has cooled, gelatin melted in water is added, and the paper is dyed in the same way as for plain or satin-colored papers. When the paper is dry, it is dyed on the other side. It is not necessary to add glazing paste. The paper is then passed between zinc rollers.

Poppy-colored. The first coat is made with yellow (see below) or orange lead. The second coat is red.

A very beautiful red paper can also be made using carmine that is ground and mixed with gelatin.

Pink. Same color, but lighter.

Yellow. Use gamboge dissolved in hot water and mixed with gelatin.

Blue. Indigo dissolved in four parts of sulphuric acid. Very fine indigo is crushed and placed in a stoneware vessel, to which sulphuric acid is added little by little, stirring with a glass spatula, and left for twelve hours in this state, after which water is added drop by drop so that the mixture does not heat up; White chalk is added in pieces to absorb the excess acid; it is drawn off and used with glue.

Lilac. Use carmine and blue.

Green. Avignon berries are boiled with alum and strained. When you want to use it, add gelatin and blue color as needed.

Green for leaves. Use a square tub, a little larger than the paper, and make a bath of green with Avignon berries and blue, according to the desired shade, with a little glue. Do not completely fill the tub. Use lightly sized paper and place it sheet by sheet on the surface of the water, then take it out and dry it. Be careful to leave each sheet in the bath for as long as possible; otherwise, the shade will be uneven. As the paper is not heavily sized, the color will soak through and color both sides.

When the paper is dry and pressed flat, it is given a coat of gum arabic on one side. The side coated with gum becomes shiny, while the other remains matte.

Paper for pulps. Take paper only colored on one side, and apply a layer of fish glue or gelatin. Sprinkle it evenly with potato starch that will stick to the glue; when the paper is dry, it will have a velvety shine, and the original color will appear transparent.

§ XIV. Neapolitan Tissue Paper for Roses

This paper is made in Naples, but the process is not well known. To make it, take some bastard saffron and put it in a cloth bag. Close it and put it in a running stream of water for a few days until no more yellow color comes out; if there is no running water, put it in a vessel filled with water and leave it. Change the water every 24 hours, squeezing the bag so the yellow water comes out. Continue to do this until the water is colorless (it takes about 6–8 days). The material will look like rotten hay. Squeeze the remaining water out of it and place it in a vessel. Sprinkle it with white potash water. Leave it for twenty-four hours, then pour some strong ordinary vinegar or wood vinegar over it. (This process will cause the dye to become pink.) Filter and store this first solution. Add vinegar to the remaining material and press it a second time. If the first solution is too strong, mix it with the second one. Keep the color covered because it will evaporate quickly.

Use a square tub, 5–7 cm (2–3 in.) deep, and the size of the paper to be dyed, which is usually tissue paper without glue. It is important to make sure that this paper is not bleached and does not have a blue tint, as this would alter the color. It is better to use natural white paper or paper that is a little yellow.

The tub is filled halfway with this color, and a sheet of paper is dipped into it. It will immediately take on a pink color. The first sheet is removed, left to drain, and hung on the strings. The same is done with the second sheet and so on. When the paper is dry, you will have a supply of paper in twenty-five shades suitable for making roses. It is necessary to take great care when handling this paper because it is very thin and will tear easily. The Neapolitans are accustomed to this manufacturing method and are skilled at it.

§ XV. Papers Printed with Woodblocks

For this kind of production, it is necessary to have a strong squared table, 2 m to 2.3 m (6–7 ft.) long and 65 cm (2 ft.) wide by 80 cm (2½ ft.) high. This table must be covered on one end, on the left, with heavy woolen cloths (diapers), with a surface of 20–22 decimeters (2 ft.) square. On the right side, a tub 65 cm (2 ft.) long, 40–45 cm (15–18 in.) wide, and 14–16 cm (5–6 in.) high is placed on a four-legged stand. In this tub, a frame is inserted, which fits exactly but can be removed and put back easily; on this frame, an oilcloth is nailed for the bottom. Smaller frames that fit into the first one are fixed with hooks to attach sheets at will because it is sometimes necessary to wash them; then, they are unhooked, washed, and put back in place.

Ordinary gum arabic, melted in water, is added to the tub and beaten so that it dissolves evenly and homogeneously. The tub must be two-thirds full; it is covered with the first frame in such a way that the bottom of this frame forms a buffer. It is necessary to take care that the canvas is well waxed and varnished so that moisture does not penetrate it (to avoid this inconvenience, it is varnished once again with greasy varnish to close all the pores better). Finally, put in this frame another frame covered with a sheet. Next to the tub, a space is left to put the bowls with the colors.

Designs of two, three, four or more colors, flowers, ornaments, arabesques, etc., are drawn and given to a wood engraver to engrave on blocks of one-half and one-quarter the size of the paper used.

All kinds of colors are used for this work; according to the design, they are adhered with starch prepared with boiling water and glazing paste (soap and wax).

To print, lay a few handfuls of paper on the table, and take color using a brush 10–15 cm (4–5 in.) long by 4–5 cm (1–2 in.) wide, and run this over the sheet of the frame well evenly, to set the color in motion; pass and repeat several times with the colored brush. Then, place the first board on it, give a few strokes to remove colors well evenly, and apply it on a waste sheet of paper to test if the color is satisfactory. If it has reached the desired shade, or if it is sufficiently dense, then the color is in good order. In this state, take some color with the board, put this board squarely on the sheet of paper by one of the top corners, and give it a few blows with a clenched fist to set the color. When the design's coverage is quite heavy, a small wooden mallet is used.

Each printing block has registration marks, usually one on each corner, which are printed at the same time as the design. When you have printed the first block, you can see on the sheet the right side mark. Take color again, and put the block on the paper a second time, placing the two left points of the block on the print of the two right points on the paper; for the third block, the two top points of the block enter the two bottom points of the first drawing, and at the fourth block your top points of this block must also correspond with those of the second and the right side with the left side of the third block.

In this stage, the sheet is put aside to dry; the second sheet is easier because the marks are already pointed and marked.

Each time the block is lifted and printed, the brush is passed over the sheet again, which is described in the section as *pulling the color*. If one has an assistant, usually an apprentice, to remove the paper and put it on the lines, then, as soon as the plate is removed, he pulls the color, and as soon as he sees that there is not enough color on the cloth frame, he puts more. If the printer notices while working that the print he has made is too light, he will make a second light print, placing the plate in the same marks as in the first print; if he sees that the plate is too heavy, he makes a print on waste paper. It often happens that the plate becomes dirty, that the small crevices are filled with color, then it is necessary to brush the plate with a brush especially used for this purpose. When you have finished printing, wash the plate with water and lay it down flat so that it doesn't work while drying.

The printer must take care to place the plate and to withdraw it well perpendicularly, not to tear the marks that the corners leave, and even not to increase them because the same reference points are used for the remaining impressions. When the paper is dry, straightened and pressed, begin the second printing; position it in the marks already established.

The engravers indicate the plates to be printed first, second and so on. It also happens sometimes that he has put there other points of reference, then he takes care to indicate their relationships.

If there is too much color on the sheet frame, it should be scraped off with a wooden scraper, and when you have finished a color, wash well, unhook the sheet from the frame, and put on another.

It is possible to print gold or silver designs with wooden boards, but a special frame of very thin and short cloth is needed; otherwise, it will have too much bite. The drawing brush must also be stiffer. Usually, a worn brush is used. (*See specimens Nos. 26 and 27.*)

You print with mordant.

№ 1. For the bronze, take boiled linseed oil and grind with half a kg (1 lb.) of this oil, 125 gm (4 oz.) of ceruse white, and 60 gm (2 oz.) orange lead, add 60 gm (2 oz.) of copal varnish, put a little with a small brush on the frame, and draw (i.e., level) with the brush to draw. Scrape and apply more until the sheet is also soaked, then take color in small quantities and print on the paper by striking a light punch, then remove the board that was put aside. Bronze powder is then taken, either white or yellow, with cotton and placed on the print that then becomes golden or silver. Usually, the designs for gilding are very light and engraved on copper or on copper and wood. It is not necessary to use too much mordant; the design would be too heavy and would not dry quickly enough.

You print with gold leaf.

№ 2. The mordant is made with half a kg (1 lb.) of very strong linseed oil and 125 grams (4 oz.) of greasy varnish with copal and siccative; 125 grams (4 oz.) of ceruse white, as much of orange lead, are ground, and one operates in the same way as with the powdered bronze. When the sheet is printed, one takes gold leaf, German gold, or beaten copper, one positions the book in one hand, and one opens a page with the other, one holds the page open, and one turns the book on the printing, the metal attaches itself on the mordant, and one raises the book: it is thus that one poses a sheet of metal one after the other and touching until the sheet of paper is entirely covered of it. One presses again a little or makes overlap a sheet on the other, and finally, one lets dry for one or two days; then one removes the not adhering metal with cotton or the paper that comes from the booklets, and one collects the shavings, which are good to make due bronze in powder.

One can also make velvety impressions when one prints with the strong mordant № 2 and that one spreads on the impression of the wool *tontisse* [flocking] pulverized very fine, that one deposited in a sieve, and that one sprinkles on the sheet placed in a case: on the opening of this case, one puts the sieve charged with wool, and one knocks in it with a bar, so that the wool passes through and falls on the sheet, in very-fine dust. This wool is attached to the printing, and when the sheet is equally well covered, it is removed and replaced by another. When the paper is quite dry, it is brushed.

As soon as the work is finished, the brush, the sheet and the floor are washed with turpentine so that the color does not dry on them. If you continue to work the next day, it would not be necessary to wash the sheet; it would be enough to scrape it well.

§ XVI. Fancy Papers Printed Using Lithography[5]

Needless to say, one needs a lithographic press, stones, rollers, and whatever else is necessary for printing. (*See specimen № 28.*)

I. Execution of the Design

The first thing to take care of is to have a drawing made, either in one or several colors, on paper. If it's a single-color drawing, you only need to make your drawing to a quarter or even a sixth or an eighth scale and then proceed to transfer it to the stone.

The draftsman must take great care to ensure that the drawing fits perfectly in all directions so that when it is transferred, the drawing is continuous without the joints being visible. It is then drawn on

---

5 A concise explanation of stone lithography can be found at www.leicesterprintworkshop.com/printmaking/ step_by_step_guide_to_stone_lithography/

a small stone with brushes or in some other way, according to the draftsman's habits.

If it's a multi-color drawing, it's best to have it completely drawn; and since this kind doesn't need to be done with great precision, this work costs no more than making transfers, which are very difficult and which, however well executed, never match up well enough, because the paper is large, needs to be wet, and therefore will stretch out in all directions. For a multi-color drawing, the draftsman makes his drawing in quarters, sixths or eighths, on plain paper. In fact, it rarely happens that we make designs the size of the sheet of paper, so we repeat it several times, and, for this reason, it's enough for it to be on a quarter, a sixth or an eighth of the size of the paper, and even a little smaller than this paper; to leave a little white margin all around.

Four, six or eight proofs are printed on the stone using transfer ink. The sheets are transferred, flush with each other, to a stone at least 3 cm (1 in.) larger than the size of the paper; marks are placed at the four corners or in the middle of each sheet; this stone is called the *impression*. As many proofs are then printed on strong paper, glued to the cylinder, as there are still colors to be done. If you have a four-color design, you need to make three transfers because one (the impression) has already been made. These prints are used to transfer the drawings onto stones. Each print is transferred to another stone, and the designer applies color to a sheet. He doesn't need to color any larger than the original drawing. He then prepares the drawing on the stones; supposing, for example, that he has a drawing requiring six colors: red, yellow, green, blue, violet and black, he then loads the stone with red in all the places that show red and violet on the sheet, in accordance with the lines due to the drawing, and he covers the marks exactly, then he takes the stone for yellow, and fills all the points indicated for yellow and green, and also puts the reference marks. After this, he takes the stone for blue and charges all the areas that are indicated for blue, violet and green, and with the fourth stone, which has already made the print, the design is complete.

Note that all fill-in is done with a quill or brush, using lithographic ink and exactly up to the lines of the sketch and that no voids are left, i.e., nothing should be left out, but none should be put in where it shouldn't be.

You only need to be a draftsman and know how to work with a quill or brush to make this kind of drawing; once a drawing has been made, the procedure is the same for the rest, and as the strokes don't need to be very delicate, you can use a fairly strong ink, provided only that it flows easily from the brush or quill, and is pure. The whole design should be continuous and shaded (cross-hatched), in the same way as a pencil drawing, and the outlines will serve as a guide for the color inlays. But once the design is finished, the proof is pulled, and the design is satisfactory, you can use a scraper to remove any areas where it is too busy or any lines or contours that are superfluous: all that is needed to succeed is a little attention, and a skilled person can, in a short time, achieve perfect designs.

II. Preparation of Lithographic Ink

A cast-iron pot of 2–4 liters capacity is filled with half a kg (1 lb.) of wax, 250 grams (8 oz.) of white Marseilles soap, which is cut into fairly small pieces, 125 grams (4 oz.) of pure tallow, and 125 grams (4 oz.) of blond shellac. All these ingredients are milled together and placed on a charcoal fire. Heat quite vigorously, stirring constantly, and when the mixture is boiling, set fire to it; then remove from the fire, leave to burn for 6–8 minutes and extinguish. Put on a tight-fitting lid to cover the pot, then extinguish the flame; in this state, add calcined lampblack until the ink is quite black. Put the flame on again and let it burn for 3–4 minutes; then extinguish, stir and pour the mass onto marble or into molds to cool. If it has been poured onto a marble, cut into pieces, and after 24 hours, the ink is dry enough to be used. However, to succeed in this operation, you need a great deal of practice, and it is best to buy your ink ready-made from merchants who have long been accustomed to making this type of ink. Lithographers also know how to prepare it very well.

To dilute this ink, take a lump of it and rub it into a cup until enough has been applied, then let a few drops of rain or river water fall on it and rub with a finger very gently, always adding more water until the ink is liquid enough, then pour it into a glass or porcelain inkwell, which is always kept covered to prevent dust from getting in. If the ink is too runny, rub it again with your finger and pour over it a little of the previous mixture already contained in the inkwell; likewise, if it is too stiff. Care must be taken not to scrub too quickly to avoid foaming.

On either side of the stone are two wooden cleats, slightly higher than the stone itself, on which a board rests so that the craftsman can rest his arms. Care must be taken not to touch the stone with the finger or hand, as the heat of the skin or the grease of the hands can cause stains. When not working, keep the stone covered.

III. The Impression

First, the paper to be transferred is prepared. Take thin paper without glue, free of bumps or small holes. Chinese paper [thin rice paper] is usually used for this purpose. Prepare some paste or glue, and filter it through a cloth so that it does not have lumps. Tint it with a little water boiled with saffron or safflower, to give it a light yellowish color. This is done to make it easier to recognize the side of the paper being prepared. Pour a little alum water into the glue. The paper is coated with this glue using a badger brush in the shape of a cod tail [i.e., a fan-shaped brush], leaving no marks or empty spaces. Hang it on a line and put it through the press to even it out when the paper is dry. Keep it clean for use. Take care not to touch it on the glued side; otherwise, it will leave indelible marks.

IV. Preparation of Transfer Ink

Place on the fire in a cast iron pot:

Strong Varnish	120 to 150	gm
Yellow wax	325	—
White soap	200	—
Pure tallow	65	—

This mixture is left to heat until it catches fire. When it has ignited, it is removed from the fire and left to burn for 4–5 minutes and then extinguished. Then, it is put back on the fire, and enough lampblack is added to make it quite black. It is lit once again and left to burn for a few minutes. It is then taken off the fire and stirred again so that all the elements are well incorporated and poured into a container for storage.

V. Preparation of Varnish for Printing

When making varnish, it's a good idea to work outdoors, as the process is very dangerous and emits a very bad odor.

Place a cast-iron pot, almost full of pure and good old linseed oil, over a good fire and heat briskly. When the oil begins to boil, add three or four peeled onions per half kg (1 lb.) of varnish, and when these onions are almost scorched or toasted, remove them and replace them with a few slices of stale bread, leave to toast, then remove, and when the oil is very hot, introduce a flame so that it catches fire; if it refuses to ignite, it's not hot enough, so you have to increase the heat; but when you see it catching fire, you have to remove it from the hearth, taking care that there's nothing left around the pot, and then leave it to flambé until the flame becomes very strong; then extinguish it with a cast-iron lid and leave it on until you are sure the flame is well extinguished; or wait a few more minutes and ignite it again; extinguish a second time in the same way as the first, and repeat this operation 4–5 times for weak varnish, 7–8 times for medium varnish, and 10–12 times for strong varnish. Leave to cool in the pot. The number of times the fire should be lit cannot be specified, as it depends on the quality of the oil, which may be more or less pure or old. If you don't need large quantities of this varnish, you're much better off buying it: it's always available from printing ink merchants in the strength you need.

VI. Preparation of the Colors

№ 1. *Calcined lampblack*. Iron or cast-iron tubes about 25–30 cm (10–12 in.) long, 10–12 cm (4–5 in.) in diameter, with one end closed and the other closed with a lid. A small hole, a few mm in diameter, is made in both the lid and the bottom. The tubes are filled with top-quality lampblack mixed with pulverized colophane rosin (125 grams to ½ kg of lampblack)[6], and the mixed black is pressed into the tube with a rounded piece of wood as firmly as possible so that it is compact and hard inside; the lid is closed tightly, and the tube is placed in the fire so that it is completely surrounded by the flame. Continue in this way until no more smoke comes out through the openings in the bottom or lid, then leave to cool in the tube itself and remove the black, which is then in pieces and kept locked up so that no dust or other matter can enter to impair its purity or quality. When we want to use it, we pulverize it and grind it with a wheel on a marble, very thick and very fine, because an important point is that all the colors are ground very fine, especially the black, which we grind very heavily so that it keeps for a long time.

№ 2. *Red*. There are three types of red in use: vermilion, Saturn red or orange lead and English red lake.

№ 3. *Blue*. For blues, Berlin blue, mineral blue and ultramarine.

№ 4. *Green*. Mix mineral blue with pale chrome yellow, or use the green known commercially as *Milori green*, which is preferable.

№ 5. *Yellow*. Pale and dark chrome yellow, natural Italian earth.

№ 6. *Brown*. Persian brown.

№ 7. *White*. Silver white.

All colors should be purchased in first quality, and only a few should be ground at a time. Vermilion is used pure, but if a yellowish red is desired, it is mixed with orange lead. All other colors are mixed with silver white. Ultramarine is used for sprinkling.

Pure Persian brown, or with very little white, gives a very beautiful chocolate brown; if you want it darker, mix it with black; for lighter brown, add white and natural Italian yellow. Adding a lot of white gives a pretty color.

Red lake makes a pink color when a lot of white is added. Red lake mixed with vermilion makes a crimson red.

6   (4 oz. to 1 lb. of lampblack)

Mineral blue with lots of white and very little carmine added gives a beautiful sky blue.

For gray, use lots of white, a little black and very little blue.

For violet or lilac, mix mineral blue, red lake and white, depending on the shade required. Ultramarine blue is used, as already mentioned, for sprinkling only.

Yellow shades, lots of varnish (medium strength) with natural Italian earth, and for gray, a little black.

All colors should be ground very finely on a hard millstone and with a glass muller, but not too hard. Red lake usually comes out hard, but when worked with the grindstone, it becomes soft and pliable again. The printer prepares in advance all the colors he believes he will need to obtain more even shades throughout the print run. The rest is put back into a pot and covered with water.

The explanations we have just given will, I think, be sufficient, and any printer with a little taste will be able to mix colors to obtain any shade he desires.

VII. Mordants

Mordant № 1. FOR BRONZE POWDER, YELLOW OR RED SHADES. Grind flake white and orange lead with medium strong varnish.

Mordant № 2. FOR SILVER BRONZE OR IMITATION SILVER. The varnish is ground with silver white.

Mordant № 3. FOR ULTRAMARINE. Grind white or mineral blue with varnish.

VIII. Execution of Transfers

When the stone leaves the hands of the designer or draftsman, and the latter has not prepared it, we take pumice stone and sand with strongly acidulated water (*acidulated water* is nitric acid diluted with water) all around this stone to remove any smudges the designer may have made on it, and to prevent the stone from taking on black in these places. Care must be taken not to touch the drawing with pumice stone or acidulated water. Dry with a clean, soft sponge, then take some weak acidulated water and test it by placing a little on one side of the stone to see if it is strong enough or too weak. This acidulated water needs to be strong enough, but not too strong so that it doesn't damage the design; this can be seen when you drop a few drops on one side of the stone, and the water doesn't damage the design but releases a few small particles. Using a soft sponge soaked in acidulated water, rub the entire stone, including the drawing, once, taking care not to miss any spots, then wash with a sponge, using pure water, and cover everything with gum dissolved in water, which is applied with a sponge and set aside to let the drawing rest under the gum for a while. The dissolved gum used should have no more consistency than a good oil.

The stone to be transferred must be smooth, free of scratches and scuffs, and well sanded with water and then dry. In hot weather, the stone should not be exposed to the sun so that it does not become hot, and in cold weather, to the air so that it does not become too cold.

Cut the paper to the size you need and place it in the fresh paper, i.e., the pre-wetted paper that you've put in the press so that it's evenly moistened and there's no more liquid water on the surface. Then, take the stone, wash it with water, and print a few proofs with black printing ink to see if everything is well prepared, after which turpentine is poured over it and wiped over with a cloth. In this state, the stone turns white, i.e., there is no more black. It is washed with a sponge soaked in fresh water, leaving only the moisture necessary for inking; take a little ink to put on the roller (the roller must be ready before removing the drawing with the spirit of turpentine) and ink the drawing, always giving a wet sponge stroke beforehand, until the drawing reappears; you must ink several times after giving the roller strokes on the inking stone. Roll until the design has completely reappeared, holding the roller firmly on the stone as you roll. When everything is in order, print a proof on the paper; ink again and print on the printing paper which has been laid between the duplicates of the fresh paper, and on the glued side, as many proofs as you need, always evenly and very cleanly and without ever touching the side to be printed with your hand, and lay it between the fresh paper. The printing paper should not be too cool; otherwise, it will stick to the stone. If it is too cool or wet, it should be left to dry a little. It's a good idea to print a few more proofs than you need so that you can choose the most uniform ones from among them. When all the proofs have been drawn, the stone is inked and laid out in greasy ink, i.e., loaded with ink to which a little tallow has been added, gummed and put aside or in its place.

Take the proofs, trim them exactly to the edges or where they need to be cut, and always put them back in the fresh paper.

A large, plain board or pasteboard is then placed on the press, and a sheet of fresh paper the size of the design is placed on top. On this sheet, place the transfer and adjust the sides exactly so that the drawing fits perfectly; prick it with a needle so that the carrier holds well on the sheet, and put the fresh paper back in between.

In this state, take the stone prepared to receive the transfer, chock it in the press to make it ready for printing, dry sand it with a fine, flat pumice stone, clean it with a clean cloth and take the paper transfer from the fresh paper and place it, of course, with the printed side on the stone. In doing so, care must be taken to ensure that the drawing is not disturbed and that it is laid square; the frame is folded down, two press strokes are given, the frame is raised, and the wet sheet is gently removed, taking care that the proofs do not come away from the stone, then the stone is turned over from top to bottom so that the side that was behind comes to the front, it is covered with another sheet of fresh paper, and two more press strokes are given. Now, the stone is moved, the paper with which it was covered is removed, and the proofs are fixed. To do this, wet the stone with a sponge and plenty of water, leave it to soak for a while, then gently remove the paper, still wetting, and all the drawing should be on the stone, with nothing left on the paper. The stone is then washed with plenty of water, without pressing, and set aside to dry, after which it is rubbed with gum and left to dry for 3–4 hours.

If the drawing is seen to be too faint, it should be left for some time, even 24 hours, without erasing, but when it is judged to be reasonably strong, it should not be left for too long without erasing; the drawing must be transferred cleanly and clearly to the stone. Sometimes, the drawing may have been duplicated because the proofs have not been sufficiently moistened and adhered to the stone by the first press stroke, in which case it must be repeated.

When the stone has been gummed for a sufficient length of time, take it back and remove the gum with a damp sponge. Take some printing ink from the ink roller, but not too much, and ink the stone very gently, keeping the roller evenly applied to the stone, which is kept very fresh. When you see that everything has gone well, proceed with the print run, but if you notice that there are places that have been missed, dry the stone so that the draftsman can retouch and mark them as well. When all is well repaired, give the stone a few strokes with a roller and prepare it with very weak acidulated water, which should hardly bite; finally, clean it with a cut feather dipped in this acidulated water to remove any stains that should not remain on the stone, put a bit of gum underneath; the retouched areas must be completely dry and remain slightly gummed, and proofs are read for the transfer, if the design is to be printed in color, but if it's a bronze or single-color design, the print can continue.

Patterns for powdered bronze should be drawn with № 1 mordant; the mordant should be kept fairly strong, and the stone should not be inked too much. Care must be taken to ensure that the strokes remain clean and free from burrs, which would show up when inking, i.e., if the mordant color were overloaded, the paper would remove everything, and the strokes would become coarse and messy. This is especially true when insufficient care is taken with a transfer stone that has not yet been removed with essence. When you've pulled 12–18 sheets, you can remove them with petrol, then ink them again. It's a good idea to ink with printing black mixed with a little transfer black and to draw a few sheets of stains. This will make the design appear stronger. With good transfer, you can often print 3–4 thousand good impressions.

Using the № 1 mordant, take some red or gold bronze powder on a cotton pad and lightly pass it over the impression several times; the impression takes on the bronze and becomes golden. If you want the design to be silvered, take № 2 mordant and apply it in the same way: when you want it to be beautiful, use powdered silver, and if it is to be more common, imitation silver.

For ultramarine, use mordant № 3, blue, and rub with ultramarine-soaked cotton. The paper is left to dry for 5–6 days and then calendered between zinc plates; gold and silver colors come out very bright. For these types of paper, we usually use glossy paper, but you can also use white paper, which is not covered with colors; only it is necessary to pass it through the calender; otherwise, the paper would pick up bronze or ultramarine, and would be difficult to clean.

For gold or silver prints (*or en feuille de cuivre battu* is the name given to beaten copper which comes from Germany; *silver leaf* is the name given to fine silver prepared in Paris), use very strong varnish, ground with silver white, or mixed with orange lead.

This mordant must be very strong, and when you begin, you must prepare it well by taking a very small quantity from the roller, which you work well on the ink table; you ink as usual, and when the sheet is pulled, you place the gold or silver leaf on top, by taking a gold book in one hand, opening it with the other hand, and turning it over the impression; in this way, the gold attaches itself to the impression, on which you apply it with cotton. When the work is finished, the printer passes the sheets through the press, taking ten or twelve at a time.

Gold or silver leaf printing is often used for embossed objects and is carried out by engraving a copper plate with a design of flowers or ornaments. The engraver makes two small holes in the plate at the top and bottom of the design. When this plate is finished, it is inked with printing ink, and a proof is made on strong, satin-finish paper. This drawing is then transferred to a stone, and the black on the surface of the plate is transferred to the stone, leaving the drawing and the two dots in white. The draftsman then fills all this white with lithograph ink, not forgetting the two small black dots, and when everything is marked and dry, it is prepared with strong acidulated water so that the black on the surface is completely removed and printed. The two small dots, which are then equally marked, serve as reference points.

Two pointed copper nails are inserted into the two small holes in the board, with the tip projecting about 2 mm, then covered with strong cardboard the size of the board and stamped with several strokes of the pendulum; the drawing must be exactly reproduced on the cardboard, and if anything is missing at certain points, small pieces of paper are glued to these points, and stamped again until the drawing is perfect. Any mistakes in the cardboard will be reproduced in the proofs, and this is something to be avoided.

The cardboard should be 7–8 mm thick and of good quality with no bumps and with a very uniform and even paste; if the cardboard is too hard, it should be placed in a damp place so that it softens a little, and when it is stamped, it should be left in the mold to dry completely. It is then stamped a second time because sometimes the moistened cardboard pulls away.

To stamp, remove the cardboard we call the *counterpart*, prick the proofs to be stamped with a needle into the small holes marked on the proofs, and place it on the two points on the board. Cover with the counterpart, evenly and equally, over the points, and insert under the balance. One or more strokes of the pendulum are then used to stamp the plate, with the designs appearing in relief on the proofs. If you're stamping on a printing press, attach the counterpart to the frame, which must be firmly fixed.

The designer should leave all objects to be colored blank so that they can be colored later with a brush, using gum color, but color proofs can be printed, and markings should be on gilt proofs. For embossing, the impressions must be very dry; otherwise, the colors remain in the hollow mold.

For color prints, the design for gold, bronze or ultramarine should be made first; similarly, it should be printed first, then the other, and if there is a background, whatever the color, it should always be printed first after the gold.

HOW TO MAKE FANCY PAPERS

The printer places the stone on the press and carefully prepares it to remove the transfer. He also cleans it with the tip of a feather and acidulated water, after which he leaves it for a while covered with gum, and in the meantime, he lays out on the table the colors he is to use according to the drawing's instructions and prepares his roller; he removes the black drawing with the essence, and prints, taking care that the marks come out well. Gold, bronze and ultramarine powder prints are made in the same way as ordinary prints, and the same procedure is followed for other prints. The black, which forms the main part of the design, should be printed last.

If the draftsman has made a mistake and it is discovered that something has been missed, the spot is sanded on the stone, a sheet of paper is taken, and the spot is filled with lithographic ink. Leave to dry, mark the sheet exactly, then give the marked spot a press; the draftsman covers it with lithographic ink, and only this spot is prepared with a paintbrush.

The register mark is then always made on the first colored print, and then the corners are cut on the left side of the stone (on the front) very exactly so that they enter clearly into the marks on the stone, and when you place on the print stone, register with great care; cover with a handguard, without being attached to the frame, so that the sheet is not disturbed, print, and give the necessary time to dry well.

Wooden rollers are used, covered with flannel and hide, one for each color, a special one for transfer and another for black. For the latter two, the reverse side of the skin is on the outside, and for the colors, it's the smooth side. When the rollers are new, they should be rolled on marble with varnish until the fluff that covers them falls off or has disappeared, and great care should be taken with them not to hit them with scrapers and to grease them with tallow when they are not in use, and then, when you want to use them, to scrape them to remove the tallow. The paper must be very strong cylinder (satin) before being printed and dry printed.

During the print run, care must be taken to ensure that the stone is very fresh and clean; always wash the color table and roller with benzine before taking on another color, as well as the wetting sponge, and that the bronze or gold leaves are laid with care.

§ XVII. Trocadéro Papers

A wide brush is prepared by nailing individual paintbrushes (with their handles cut off) side-by-side. Use brushes measuring 12–15 mm in diameter up to a width of 3–4 cm to a lath measuring 45 cm (18 in.) long, and cover it with another lath of the same size. Prepare the color by mixing with ceruse white and some hide glue (the glue ensures that the paint is slightly thick). Always mix white alone. Lay the paper lengthwise in front of you, and place the colors you wish to use in small vases beside it; each vase should hold a finger-sized brush.

A small brushful of color is placed on the first section of the wide brush you made previously, in the middle of the blue, on the second tail yellow, on the third red, on the fourth white, and so on along the length of the brush. This brush is applied to the top end of the paper and drawn towards you in a straight line by applying the brush tips to the paper and pulling—without wavering the hand—and without leaving the sheet. If you don't have enough color in the brush, load it with more color in exactly the same spot and repeat until the colors are close together. In this state, they blend together, and the result is a shade of red, lilac, blue, green, yellow, orange, red, pink and white. By changing the colors, other shades can be obtained. When the brush is sufficiently soaked, there's no need to pick up several colors at a time, and if these colors mix too much, they should be washed and dried before starting again. Flawed sheets, or the first ones made, are used for the backgrounds of Polish or other marbled papers. This process can be simplified by using two colors. (*See Specimen № 29.*)

§ XVIII. Papers with Images or Sanctity
[*Papiers a images ou de sainteté*]

Plates are engraved using either a tin plate or a wood block. This kind of artwork must be engraved with wide lines. Put on a letterpress, and ink lightly with mordant № 2. Cover the mordant with gold or silver leaf. After a few days, when this leaf is dry, rub it to remove the loose material, and, to make it more beautiful, it is again put on the same plate, in exactly the same place, and it is printed without the mordant, i.e., on the dry plate, using strong pressure. Through this operation, the gold becomes brighter and gives a more brilliant appearance. Fine etchings and very beautiful patterns can be made this way. To give a sharper look, they can be lightly embossed with a design. (*See specimen № 29.*)

§ XIX. Gilded or Silvered Paper

Plate. A plate is the layer of color that covers the paper.

To prepare this plate, grind 1½ kg (3 lbs.) of greasy, heavy pipe clay with half a kg (1 lb.) of red bole and 60 grams (2 oz.) of English graphite. (Grind everything very finely.) Add 1½ kg (3 lb.) of hide glue. Pass the mixture through a sieve; use paper that is well-sized, smooth, and without lumps, and give it two even coats with this plate; let the paper dry and then press flat.

Melt 125 grams (4 oz.) of Flanders glue in a liter of water, add 30 grams (1 oz.) of white honey, and leave to cool. This glue should remain liquid when cold but still be sticky. Check this by taking a little between two fingers and testing whether it sticks or not.

Place the paper coated with the plate on a table or desk that is large enough to allow some space around the paper. Using a 4–5 cm badger shaving brush, cover the entire sheet with a layer of the above-mentioned Flanders glue solution; start at the top and work your way down so the paper is well soaked in the glue. Place gold, silver, copper or imitation gold leaf, one sheet against the other; place on a line to dry quickly; then clean and smooth the paper's surface. (*See specimens № 31 and № 32.*)

You can also make gold and silver paper by taking white paper and applying a layer of glue prepared with honey, then sprinkling it with bronze powder and smoothing it out. Finally, you can even use gold powder that has been passed through a very fine sieve.

In 1844, Monsieur Lapeyre took out a patent for colored papers, which are manufactured as follows: The papers used in this case are the dark, satin or glazed papers used for wall hangings and fancy papers.

A thin glue, lightly tinted with a color opposite to that of the background, is applied to these prepared backgrounds using the hand and a brush to create transparency and a second nuance. While the glue is still wet, a very fine silk sieve containing fake gold or tin powder is sprinkled on top of the glue, which attaches to the background through the still-wet glue, adding a third gold or silver shade to the previous two and helping to melt them. Once the papers are dry, they are polished with a stone from the back, uniting everything and allowing the flecks of false gold or pewter to shine through, bringing out the different shades.

For the same non-colored papers, darkening and smoothing are carried out on unprepared white papers.

§ XX. Metallic Moiré Papers

Use silver paper prepared in the manner previously indicated and without being polished. Take some color that is sized with hide glue. Put a little of this color on a board, rub it with a sponge that is not too fine, and then touch the silver side of the paper with this sponge and let it dry. It is polished. The areas the sponge did not touch are shiny, while the areas with the color has set remain transparent.

§ XXI. Imitation Donkey Hide

Take strong papers, and on both sides, give them two heavy coats of color with ceruse white bonded with hide glue. To give them a yellowish tone, add a bit of ochre. When the paper is dry, apply another coat using ceruse white crushed with linseed oil. After they have dried, pass them through the roller. You can write on this paper with pencils and then erase the marks.

§ XXII. Imitation Slate

Take some clinker[slag] produced by blacksmiths during their forging and crush it very finely. Grind it with unboiled linseed oil and apply several coats of this to strong paper. To do this, take a brush and apply the color evenly to the paper, then scrub it in as deeply as possible with a felt pad until the color is almost dry; this operation is repeated several times on both sides of the paper until enough color is visible, then take some dry powdered clinker and rub it in to absorb the oil completely. Leave it to dry. One can write as well with a slate pencil on this imitation slate paper as on a natural slate.

§ XXIII. Metallic Paper

In England, a paper for notebooks was invented and named *metallic paper* because it is written on with pencils made of a metallic alloy composed of three parts of tin, two of lead, three of bismuth, and one of mercury (quicksilver).

One-half kg (1 lb.) of zinc white and 125 grams (4 oz.) of calcined deer horn (lime phosphate) are ground with water and glued with 1½ kg (3 lb.) of white hide glue, and 1 kg (2 lb.) of starch glue (blue starch). To give the paper a bluish tint, add a few drops of an indigo solution or a little Prussian blue paste. Lightly and evenly coat both sides of the paper. It is finished by passing between the cylinders.

This paper can be made more simply by taking very fine powdered zinc white and wiping it over the paper with a cloth rag. The paper must be well glued or glued beforehand and then Calendered.

§ XXIV. Sketch Paper for Pastels

Pumice stones are ground fine; this powder is then washed and decanted to make it finer, and if the paper is to be dyed yellow, gray, or bluish, this powder is stained with Italian earth, black or indigo liquor, allowed to dry, and then it is powdered.

The adhesive is made with half a kg (1 lb.) of strong glue melted in 3–4 liters of water, and then 60 grams (2 oz.) of honey is added. Coat the paper with a layer of this. Sprinkle immediately. Before the glue is completely dry, put the pumice powder through a fine sieve and pass it evenly over the entire surface of the sheet. The powder will stick to the glue. When the paper is dry enough, the pumice that is not attached is removed. It is easy to paint with pastels. Several grades of fineness can be made by using pumice powder that is more or less fine.

Congrève's Printing Method

About twenty years ago, a way was sought in England to emulate or rather to counterfeit the bills of English currency or *banknotes*. It was then that Guillaume Congrève invented this method of printing, which was also adopted for prints, labels, book covers, etc. It is carried out today in various large establishments and has even been used in various countries for printing currency.

§ I. Description of Engraved Printing Plates

Take two boards bearing the same design or engraving and carve out one of them, as indicated on the design, with a carving tool. Then, take the second board and cut out the places or parts of the design that are missing or have been removed from the first so that it fits perfectly with your first board. Place the board thus adjusted on a hard wooden board of the same size, 20–25 mm thick, and glue the small pieces cut from the second board to the wooden one using wax to which you have added a little tar and varnish; attach to the first board, on each side, a handle by which you can easily remove and reattach it. Great care must be taken in this work, both in cutting and in fitting, so that when the boards are joined together, they form a single unit. This can be used to make any kind of engraving, guilloché, or lettering. Letters and hollows are added to the engraving to create relief. In England, Mr. Whiting of London and in Germany, Mr. Haenel of Berlin use presses also invented by Mr. G. Congrève, but which are extremely expensive. Everywhere else, we use a strong Stanhope press, with double or single levers, and a *presse à balancier* for relief objects.

For the solder, the Darcet's alloy is used. It is composed of:

> 5 parts tin,
> 3 parts lead, and
> 8 parts bismuth.

§ II. Preparation of the Colors

Once the board has been assembled, it's time to prepare the colors.

In the beginning, copahu balsam was used to grind the colors, but this material is very expensive and has a very bad odor. Today, we use linseed oil varnish, the same as that used for lithography, to which we add 65 grams (2 oz.) of white Marseilles soap for every half kg (1 lb.) of varnish (the soap is grated off and melted into the hot varnish). All colors need to be well ground, and white can be added; it should even be added because this white will cover quite a lot.

Gelatin rollers are used, like letterpress rollers, but they must not be too hard, and when not in use, they are hung in a cool place to prevent them from drying out.

The rolling table is made of marble or lithographic stone because these materials can be washed and kept very clean. You can't be too clean in this kind of work, and you must always thoroughly wash when changing color. The paper must be fresh but not too damp.

§ III. Colors

№ 1. *Red.*   1. Vermilion.

2. Vermilion with ¼ English red lake for crimson.

3. Carmine red lake with $1/16$ silver white.

4. Orange lead for shading to orange.

5. English lake with six parts white for *rose.*

№ 2. *Dark blue.* Pure Berlin blue.

№ 3. *Medium blue.* Pure mineral blue or very little silver white.

№ 4. *Sky blue.* Mineral blue, much silver white.

№ 5. *Lighter blue.* Mineral blue, bismuth white.

№ 6. *Green*. Milori green, to which pale chrome yellow and white are added, depending on the shade to be produced.

№ 7. *Light yellow*. One part chrome yellow, and three to four parts silver white.

№ 8. *Dark yellow*. Orange lead is added according to shade.

№ 9: *Nankeen yellow*. Natural Italian earth, with white.

№ 10. *Brown, reddish-brown*. Caput mortuum, also known as *Vandyke brown* or *Persian brown*.

№ 11. *Dark brown*. Made with Indian red and black, with more or less natural Italian earth or white added.

№ 12. *Brown-black*. Variable proportions of black are added.

№ 13. *Violet*. Mineral blue, carmine red lake and silver white.

№ 14. *Gray*. Silver white, a little black and very little blue.

№ 15. *Black*. Printer's black.

It is very easy to formulate any color in any shade.

§ IV. Printing

To ink, remove the first plate, place it sideways on a table between two small rails to prevent the roller from slipping, and load it with color by passing the roller over it. After this, we ink the board in the press, or second board, with another color and place the first, which fits exactly, on top of the second. Then, cover with paper, lower the frame, and pull, holding the handle a moment to let the color set.

Large sheets can be printed in this way; if there are several designs to be printed, they are fused close together very precisely. Or you can make clichés and print as many repeats as the sheet will hold. Of course, all these plates must be equal in height and exactly adjusted. The work can also be aided by adding shims, as in letterpress printing. Usually, there are two people at the press, one inking the first color, the other the second.

You can also print in three, four or more colors, but for each color you need a plate that can be removed and fitted into the others; only the last one remains fixed in the press. A frisket can be used to keep the paper clean. Don't apply too much pressure.

§ V. Printing Borders and Frames

The same method can be used to produce embossed prints for signs, boards, advertisements, etc.

The names of items or objects of any kind are engraved on a tin plate or in letterpress type, and the main object is surrounded by fillets in strips of different shapes, followed by explanations or details in small characters without a frame. The strips are then cut between two of these fillets, using a cutting saw, and placed together on a wooden board; beforehand, the reverse side of the strips is coated with mastic prepared with wax, tar and varnish. In this state, the whole is placed on a press. The frame is folded down, and the lever is pulled. When the frame is raised, the board remains fixed and is thus loaded with the strips that now adhere to it. There's no need to remove the board; just cover it with two sheets of thin, glued paper or fog paper, and take a paste made with half yellow wax and half powdered Meudon white. Heat this paste until it is workable, spread it evenly on board-sized sheets, leave to cool so that the paste is still hot enough to press easily into the hollows of the engravings, cover with strong paper onto which wax has been passed from behind, and cover with the chassis. This wax paste proof is then fixed to the frame, and we examine whether everything has come out well. If any unevenness is found, or if there are places on the plate where the impression has failed, these places are filled with wax paste, covered with pieces of paper and pressed again. If the whole is no longer hot enough, we heat it up, taking some old paper, which we roll and light, bringing it close to the paste, which soon becomes hot enough again; then we press harder, and if everything comes out well, we cut the wax paste that has come out of this counterpart, so that it is no larger than the engraved plate; we let it cool, and in the meantime, we prepare the colors, as indicated above.

These signs can be printed in several colors, with each panel printed in a certain shade and the background also in a different color.

For example, if there are three panels, you can print the top one in blue, the middle one in yellow, the third in red, and the background in brown or green, giving you four colors, with the letters standing out white and in relief. The large plate can also be engraved with an ornamental or arabesque border, which will be white on any background.

A border can also be made separately, in a different color, but this border must be engraved separately, and the plate adjusted exactly in the frame, but in such a way that the frame can be removed to ink it separately; this frame must be adjusted before proceeding with the counterpart.

We usually have different frames fixed on wood, which are the same height as the board being placed inside and which serve as a *passe-partout* frame.

Varnishing Colored Prints and Fancy Papers

For a few years, colored prints and fancy papers have been varnished. We will describe the processes for this operation.

Two formulas are used for this varnishing: one with shellac and the other with gelatin.

§ I. Varnishing with Shellac

Take one liter of the highest grade spirit of wine; at least 36° B [36° C, 97° F], and add 200 grams (6 oz.) of white shellac and 65 grams (2 oz.) of mastic pearls. Subject to a heat of 10–15 degrees in a well-stoppered bottle for 3–4 days. Shake the bottle several times a day, and the varnish will be ready at the end of this time.

Take the sheets to be varnished and paste them with gelatin. To do this, melt 125 grams (4 oz.) of gelatin in one liter of water, add 7–8 grams (about ¼ oz.) of white soap and let it cool. If the glue is too stiff, add more water. This glue should be slightly set when it is cold. It can be renewed by heating on a very low fire. With a brush, lightly apply the glue to the sheets to be varnished and stretch them over the lines until they are completely dry. Then, pass them through cylinders between zinc plates to give them a satin finish.

Take wood planks 65 cm (2 ft.) wide, by 2 m to 2.5 (6–8 ft.) long, covered with zinc. It is good if these planks are slightly rounded. Take the sheets to be varnished, and use a small brush to draw a thin line of either strong dissolved gum or strong glue very close to the edge, and glue them side by side on the board. Apply pressure with a blade so that they do not overlap and become thick. When dry, polish them with a buffer the way a cabinetmaker varnishes furniture—with a buffer loaded with shellac varnish. To make it slide, use a little olive oil. Polish until the sheets are rather brilliant.

§ II. Varnishing with Gelatin

Take polished glass of a good thickness and place it in frames 2–3 cm thick and a little larger than the sheets to be varnished. This glass must be centered in the middle of the frame so that the varnish cannot enter the assembly.

Melt strong Flanders glue, or white gelatin, at the rate of half a kg (1 lb.) to eight liters of water, strain through a cloth so that nothing unsavory remains and let it cool a little. In the meantime, moisten the sheet on the uncolored side with a sponge. Use a cloth to spread ox gall evenly on the perfectly clean glass. Then, spoon the melted gelatin into the center of the glass and spread it over the entire surface to form an even layer. Place it on a level table. Take the damp sheet, lay it down on the glass, starting in one corner so that the paper will lay in the gelatin evenly, and roll it down slowly so as not to leave pinholes.

Pressure is applied with the wet sponge while laying the paper down. Check the other side for pinholes when the sheet is entirely laid down. If there are any, prick them with a needle to make the air go out of them. Put this aside to dry a little, and when the paper is half dry, look at it; if you see that the glue is sticking to the frame, detach it so that the sheet can be removed more easily. When the whole thing is dry, the sheet will fall off by itself. If there are places where it sticks, then there was no gall on that spot.

OTHER ITEMS

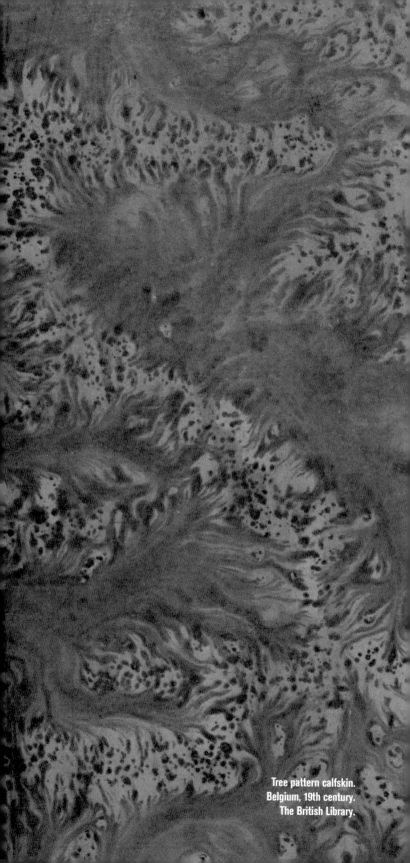

Tree pattern calfskin.
Belgium, 19th century.
The British Library.

Sealing Wax

In all the books that discuss industrial chemistry, the manufacture of sealing wax is discussed, and in general, the procedures described are exact and correct, but they are not geared to achieving the actual objective because to manufacture for one's own use is a very different thing than to do so commercially. In the first case, the aim is only to obtain a good product, while in the second, the product must have a pleasing appearance and, importantly, be manufactured at a reasonable cost. To achieve this aim, one must combine the precepts of chemistry—the recommendations from texts—and the practical application. For this reason, we will give the formulas based on the principles of chemistry and then the practical applications.

§ I. Theoretical Formulas
№ 1. Red Wax

Vermilion

Venetian turpentine[1]

Shellac flakes

Spanish white (chalk)

Bone ash (lime phosphate)

Turpentine spirits and colophane rosin

Fragrances, balsam of Tolu from Peru, liquid styrax, benzoin, or essence of clove, musk, or rosemary essence

---

1 *Venetian turpentine* is a thick, honey-like resin. It is still produced by Sennelier, Maimeri, and Richeson.

№ 2. Black Wax

Lampblack

Shellac flakes

Venetian turpentine

Turpentine spirits

Colophane rosin

Spanish white or bone ash

Fragrance

№ 3. Golden Wax

Venetian turpentine

Shellac flakes

Dragon's blood[2]

Bronze powder

Fragrance

№ 4. Colored Waxes

Blonde and white shellac flakes

Venetian turpentine

Turpentine spirits

Bismuth white (oxide)

Bone ash

Prussian blue

Ultramarine

Carmine lake

Dragon's blood

Green cinnabar or Milori green

Chrome yellow

Royal yellow or orpiment

Caput mortuum (Vandyke brown)

Vandyke brown

Vermilion

Fragrance

---

2   *Dragon's blood* is a bright red resin.

§ II. Utensils

- A large bowl or tub
- Various earthenware pans and cast iron lids
- A stove to melt, and a stove to heat the plates
- A marble table
- Wooden spatulas for stirring
- Copper and marble molds
- A press for the copper molds
- Stamps for marking
- A press for marking
- A board for rolling the sticks
- Scales and weights
- A table knife
- Gauze to press the material through
- A large earthenware or marble dish for mixing ingredients

§ III. First Step: Washing the Turpentine

In a large bowl or tub, take a portion of Venetian turpentine (or use Swiss or Austrian turpentine, which are clear and transparent and do not need to be washed). Put it under the water spout, pour in water, and wash it while you beat it with a large, stiff wooden spatula. This operation is repeated until the material becomes white and as much water as possible has been removed. It is left to rest, and the water that has come to the surface is removed again.

Take some Spanish white in the earthen or marble dish, speckle it with turpentine, knead it with your hands and a small spatula to turn it into a paste weighing about 250 grams (8 oz.), and cover it so that the mixture does not dry. It is not necessary to prepare too much in advance; otherwise, the turpentine evaporates. At most, you should only make enough for one day.

Before moving on to the description of the molding and other operations, we will give the proportions for each number, as they are generally marked in the trade.

§ IV. Proportions of Ingredients
Red Wax

№ 00   Turpentine. . . . .   ½   kg

Blonde shellac flakes 1   —

German Vermilion. . . . . .1½   —

Bone ash . . . .   ¼   —

Balm of Tolu or other fragrance, according
to the taste of your consumer   65   gm
(We suggest balsam of Tolu.)

№ 0   Turpentine. . . . .   ½   kg

Blonde shellac. 1   —

Vermilion . . . . .1¼   —

Bone ash and fragrance. . . . .   ½   —

№ 1   Turpentine. . . . .   ¾   kg

Blonde shellac. 1   —

Vermilion 1   —

Bone ash and fragrance. 1   —

№ 2   Venetian turpentine, unwashed . . . .   ¾   kg

Shellac. 1   —

Vermilion . . . .   ¾   —

Spanish white . . . . .1½   —

№ 3   Venetian turpentine. 1   kg

Shellac. 1   —

Vermilion . . . .   ¾   —

Spanish white 2   —

№ 4   Venetian turpentine. 1   kg

Shellac. 1   —

Vermilion . . . .   ½   —

Spanish white . . . . .2½   —

№ 5	Venetian turpentine	1	kg
	Colophane rosin	¼	—
	(You can also use white resin.)		
	Shellac	1	—
	Vermilion	½	—
	Spanish white	3½	—

№ 6	Venetian turpentine	1	kg
	Shellac	1	—
	Vermilion	3/8	—
	Colophane rosin or white resin	½	—
	Spanish white	4½	—

№ 7	Venetian turpentine	1	kg
	Shellac	1	—
	Colophane rosin or white resin	1	—
	Vermilion	3/8	—
	Spanish white	6	—

№ 8	Venetian turpentine	1	kg
	Shellac	1	—
	White resin	2	—
	Vermilion	¼	—
	Spanish white	7½	—

§ V. Manufacture

Take an earthenware pot of 2 to 3 liters, suitable to be exposed to the action of fire without danger. Pour in the turpentine and place it on a good charcoal fire, which should not be too hot because this must be heated slowly. Soon, the material will begin to steam and boil due to the effect of the water contained in it. Stir with a wooden spatula, but be careful not to splash it on your hand because you would be badly burned. While there is still a lot of water in it, the turpentine rises, then it must be removed from the fire until it has settled. It is put back on the fire until it no longer has this rising effect. Then, the shellac is added little by little, constantly stirring. When everything is well melted, the bone ash, which has been pulverized into a fine powder, is added and kneaded with turpentine. Then, the vermilion is added. Stir so that it is perfectly mixed.

Take another smaller earthenware pot with a long and slender spout so that you can pour more easily into the molds. Cover the pot with a piece of cloth, tie it with string, and pour the shellac, turpentine and white mixture over it, stirring to make it pass through the cloth. If this mixture is not hot enough, it is heated a little, and when everything is through, the material remaining on the cloth is scraped off with a knife; that which is beneath is unfit for manufacture; it is discarded or put aside, and that above is added with the material in the pan and put back on the fire to heat a little. The fragrances are added, and in fine qualities, Nos. 00, 0, 1, where there is not much white, a little turpentine is added before the fragrances; a little simmer is given, and it is poured into the mold, placing the pan alongside, but not on the fire.

The molds for the oval sticks are made of copper and are each for six sticks. They are made in two parts, each representing one half of the stick and open at the top and bottom. They are placed in a wooden press, with a screw and separations on each side, so that six to eight molds can be placed, two by two, one against the other, and placed upright on a marble table. The molds are tightened so that they are well joined, and they are filled by pouring through the opening. Small openings are formed on the top of the stick when they are full. These are filled and cut evenly with a knife. The molds are removed and opened; at the corner of each mold, a slot is made to insert a knife and facilitate opening. We proceed, when the molds are opened, to polish and mark, as we will explain later, and after having spoken about another way of working, which is the following:

To make flat, half-round or square sticks, we have a marble mold of a size to hold from 12 to 30 sticks and even more, depending on the size of the sticks we want to make, which are usually 8, 12, 16, 20, or 24 to the half kg This mold or form is made of solid, fine-grained marble, and black is the best for this purpose. One takes a marble stone 6–8 cm

(2–3 in.) thick and of a size proportionate to the number of sticks one wishes to cast in it and has it hollowed out to such a depth that one can, in the same hollows, cast in several increments, i.e., 8–12 or 12–16 to the half kg The maker must be trained to practice pouring and know at which height it must fill the hollows for such and such weight of the sticks. The mold is then placed straight and plumb on a table and poured in. The sticks are immediately cold enough to be extracted and placed on a marble table; when they are cold, they can be stacked on top of each other. These sticks are already polished to half their height, so they only need to be buffed on the side that was in the mold.

There are two methods to polish and mark the sticks of wax.

First method. For the oval sticks, the mold is opened and the two sides are separated. For that, one uses a knife that one inserts at the corner in the top of the mold. A part of the sticks remains attached on one of the sides and the other part on the other side. Sometimes, all the sticks adhere to one side; only one side of the mold is taken with full hand, and it is held on a fire of coal, the same on which it is melted and heated until the sticks are brilliant, then the mark is applied, and one takes thereafter the other portion which one treats in the same way, and so on. The sticks are removed and laid flat on the marble table, where they are left to cool; the material remaining in the pan is then heated, and a small amount of turpentine is added for another pouring. When the molds become too hot, they must be immersed in cold water to cool them and dried with a cloth. When the sticks are cold, they are piled up, but they are still polished only on one side; to polish them on the other side, some of them are taken in hand and held over hot coals until they become shiny on that side, and they are placed on the marble to cool.

Second method. We have an oven or large furnace, spacious enough to heat a few iron rods 15–16 cm (5–6 in.) in length.

We have three or four iron bars with iron shanks and wooden handles; put these irons on the furnace so that they turn red. While they are heating, the wax is placed on the marble table, one stick next to the other, and when the iron bars are glowing, they are passed over the sticks, 5 or 6 cm (2 to 3 in.) away, until the sticks become shiny. They are marked, and the same procedure is followed for the remaining sticks.

§ VI. Colored Sealing Waxes

№ 1. *Crimson Red*

Venetian turpentine, washed. . . . . .½	kg
White shellac 1	—
Vermilion .1	—
Carmine lake. . . . . .¼	—
Dragon's blood powder 65	gm
Bismuth white. . . . . .½	kg
Fragrance	

№ 2. *Pink*

Venetian turpentine, washed. . . . . .½	kg
White shellac 1	—
Carmine lake. . . . . .¼	—
Bismuth white. 1	—
Fragrance	

If you want darker pink shades, put more carmine lake in them, and if you want lighter, more white.

№ 3. *Dark Blue*

Venetian turpentine. . . . . .½	kg
Blonde shellac. 1	—
Berlin blue, first quality . . . . $3/8$	—
Bismuth white. . . . . .¼	—
Fragrance	

№ 4. *Sky Blue*

Spirits of turpentine . . . . .½	kg
White shellac 1	—
Berlin blue. . . . . .¼	—
Bismuth white. 1	—
Fragrance	

№ 5. Light Blue

Venetian turpentine, washed. . . . . ½		kg
White shellac 1		—
Ultramarine from Germany . . . . ½		—
Bismuth white. . . . . ½		—
Fragrance		

№ 6. Lilac

Mix together sky blue wax and pink wax.

№ 7. Dark Green

Venetian turpentine. . . . . ½		kg
Blonde shellac. 1		—
Green cinnabar, or Milori Green. . . . . ½		—
Berlin blue. 65		gm
Bone ash . . . . ½		kg
Fragrance		

№ 8. Light Green

Venetian turpentine. . . . . ½		kg
Blonde shellac. 1		—
Green cinnabar, or Milori Green. . . . . ½		—
Royal yellow 150		gm
Bone ash 65		—

You can change this shade by adding a little blue or more yellow.

№ 9. Yellow

Spirits of Turpentine . . . . ½		kg
Blonde shellac. 1		—
Spôner's chrome yellow or ½ kg of Royal yellow or orpiment . . . . ³/₈		—
Bone ash . . . . ½		—
Fragrance		

If using chrome yellow, you can add a little more bone ash. If you want to make dark yellow, you may add a little red wax; if you're going to make orange wax, use half yellow and half red. Yellow wax made with chrome yellow is more beautiful but becomes a bit grayer when glossy.

№ 10. Gray

Venetian turpentine, washed. . . . . .½	kg
White shellac 1	—
Bone ash 1	—

A little lampblack and blue, depending on the shade
Fragrance

№ 11. Brown

Venetian turpentine. . . . . .½	kg
Blonde or red shellac 1	—
Vandyke brown . . . . .¾	—
Bone ash . . . . .¼	—

Fragrance

The shade can be changed by adding red, yellow, or black. A beautiful brown can also be made by using dragon's blood instead of the Vandyke brown at a weight of 250 or 750 grams (8 or 12 oz.). This wax becomes transparent.

№ 12. Golden Wax

Venetian turpentine. . . . . ³⁄₈	kg
Red shellac. .1	—
Bronze powder, № 10 to № 20 . . . . —
Golden color 125–200	gm

Fragrance

If you add a few decagrams of dragon's blood, the color will become brown.

№ 13 *White*

Venetian turpentine, washed	½	kg
White shellac	1	—
Bismuth white	1¼ to 1½	—
Fragrance		

Add a little blue to give a soft azure tone.

№ 14 *Black*

Venetian turpentine	½	kg
Blonde shellac	1	—
Lampblack	½	—
Bone ash	¼	—
Fragrance		

Adding Spanish white or bone ash in greater proportion will result in an inferior quality result.

In all the colors where there is not a lot of white that one can mix with turpentine, one adds a little turpentine before molding so that they are more liquid, but one must first give them a boil to evaporate the turpentine, and then add more fragrance.

The molding process is precisely the same as for the red. If you want to make marbled shades, put a few small pieces of the other colors at the end of the spout of the mold and heat them so they adhere. Then, they melt when you pour and flow with the mass of the wax, where they form the marbling.

It is also possible to roll the wax instead of pouring it; in this case, the material is taken with a wooden spatula and cooled on a marble. The wax is weighed to make 2 to 3 sticks, depending on the number of sticks per half kg, and kneaded until it is suitable for rolling and modeling. It is rolled with the hand to the length of 2 to 3 sticks and leveled with a wooden board; when it is finished rolling, it is drawn to length and polished over hot coals. Finally, it is marked for lengths, and when it is cold, it is broken in the marked places to make the sticks.

§ VII. Sealing Wax with Ornaments, Arabesques, Flowers, etc.

Oval wax sticks 2½ cm (1 in.) longer than ordinary sticks are molded and rolled. It is necessary to have a press of the same size as a stamp press and a mold made like a wax stick, having two sides and closing at the top. The top and bottom sides are engraved with ornaments, etc. The top side fits over the screw of the press so that it cannot turn and fits exactly over the bottom mold. It is important that the mold can be easily put on and taken off the press to insert the stick and remove it when it is impressed.

The wax stick is then taken in the tip of a small pair of tongs and heated over a charcoal fire, turning it so that it heats all around. Care must be taken to raise its temperature enough to press and mark it, but the heat must not be raised too high; otherwise, it would be impossible to remove it from the mold.

One can also make stamped wax in which the ornaments are in bronze or in colors. For bronze, red, yellow or white bronze is put into the hollow of the mold with a small brush, and it then adheres to the wax. For colored ornaments, watercolors are applied in the same way as for coloring engravings.

§ VIII. General Rule

The weight of turpentine used in the formula of the waxes cannot be measured precisely because it depends on the quality and nature of the shellac. Sometimes a little more is needed, and sometimes a little less. This proportion also depends on the degree to which the washed turpentine is free of water. The safest thing to do when dealing with another type of shellac is to try it out and then establish the proportions. All the colors introduced into the wax must be finely powdered.

One can also make sealing wax for bottles or packages with ordinary turpentine, resin, and Spanish white, dyed with vermilion, Prussian red, black, yellow and green. The manufacturer can easily establish his standards and set his prices according to the conditions he finds himself in.

Sealing Wafers

§ I. Paste Sealing Wafers

It is necessary to have an oven with an opening 1 m (3 ft.) long, 32 cm (1 ft.) wide; on the front, this oven is provided with a door to introduce the wood or the coal; there are at the top two bars for the irons to rest on.

There must be at least three irons, made like waffle or wafer irons, 18 to 20 cm (8 to 9 in.) long and 14 to 16 cm (5 to 6 in.) wide, oval, well-polished inside, and very well adjusted.

In a large bowl, 2 to 3 kg (4 to 6 lb.) of flour are mixed with water, and the following colors are added—having been crushed with water.

For. . . red . . . . vermilion
For. . . pink . . . . red lake
For. . . blue. . . . . Prussian blue
For. . . green. . . . . Prussian blue and chrome
or stil de grain
For. . . yellow . . . . chrome yellow or
stil de grain
For. . . white. . . . . nothing
For. . . black . . . . Frankfurt black
For. . . brown . . . . Prussian red, with or
without black

The color is added until the desired shade is obtained, and it is mixed with the flour by using a wooden spoon until no dry flour is left;

water is added if it becomes too thick because it must flow easily from a spoon.

In the meantime, the irons are heated; when they are hot enough, they are rubbed inside with a cloth to which a little yellow wax has been applied, and they are wiped with another clean cloth. Then, pour some mixture on one side of the iron that has been placed flat on the edge of the stove, fold the other one on top, clamp the tongs at the end and place it on the middle bar. Fill another iron of the same shade as the first; take this one, cut the material that came out with a knife, turn it over and try to see if the material is well-baked. If it is, the iron should open easily; if it does not open, the iron is not hot enough. If it does not open, the iron is not hot enough. Then, a third iron can be filled: everything depends on the level of heat (the iron's heat that can not be measured). The worker in charge of heating the irons must observe the degree of heat he needs to work with two or three irons. A skilled worker can work with four irons. The iron should not be too greasy; otherwise, the material will slide out of the iron.

When the wafers are baked, they are put in a basket and taken to a cellar so that they can absorb the moisture they need to be trimmed to the desired size.

When the wafers have become moist enough, cut them by taking 3 or 4, sticking them by the edge one on the other in several points and putting them on a table made of well-finished basswood; cut them with a round punch of the desired size. This punch is placed on the edge, the hand is placed on the handle, which is rounded, and the iron is pressed while turning until the iron has passed through the 3 or 4 wafers. The iron is lifted, and the same operation is repeated successively. The wafers in the middle are brighter than those on the outside. When everything is cut, the punch is emptied.

§ II. Transparent Sealing Wafers

Operate in the same way as in preparing gelatin for prints, except that the plates or frames do not need to be as large. They are washed with ox gall, and a little more glue is put on the glass to strengthen the tablet.

One does not even need gelatin; one can use a clear, strong glue from Alsace. In addition, one may dye it. For red, use a decoction of Fernambouc wood and alum; for purple, use brazilwood and alum; for yellow, use yellow wood and alum or use Avignon berries; for blue, use indigo liquid; for green, combine blue and yellow. When the tablets are half dry, they are detached around the frame with a knife. When they are dry, they will detach themselves from the glass. Do not place them in a damp place before cutting; the tablets will lose their shine. They are cut in the same way as the flour ones, but one by one.

The same method can be used to make frosted paper for transferring engravings. White glue or gelatin can be made in any size, depending on the number of sheets of glass available, as well as gelatin printing plates for address cards, business cards or other objects. The impression of a mordant and bronze on these cards is very elegant.

Mouth Glue

Half a kg (1 lb.) of Flanders glue is melted in 4 liters of water; 125 grams (4 oz.) of sugar (brown sugar) is added. When the mixture is half-cooled, it is poured on a smooth marble slab surrounded by a frame so that the material cannot flow out and the sheets are of uniform thickness. Pour to the desired thickness, and when the sheets are almost dry, cut them with a chisel into small tablets 2–3 cm (1 in.) wide by 6–7 cm (2–3 in.) long, and let them dry. This glue must be kept in a dry place.

Pencils

Graphite pencils have been known since the middle of the previous century. In the old days, artists used black stone or red chalk, as well as charcoal for drawing, until a Capuchin in an Italian convent invented a composition that consisted of graphite powder mixed with colophane, which he rolled into small sticks and made to fit into canes. These pencils were of inferior quality, brittle and did not mark well. Later, pencils were made in England and Nuremberg, Bavaria. In England, they are made only with natural graphite found in the province of Cumberland, which is the best substance that can be used to make pencils. This graphite is soft, soapy and shiny, very fine and tightly grained, not sandy, and its iron veins are so evident that it is not difficult to remove them. But this graphite is not very abundant. It is also used for the treatment of skin diseases; the government has prohibited its export under the most severe penalties. It even keeps the key to the mine so that the owner can only extract a small portion each year, part of which is sold to pharmacists and the rest is used to make pencils. These pencils are, therefore, very expensive, and this incentive to cheat has not been lacking. Pencils have been made which were thought to be of good quality, but when they were sharpened, they were found to have 12–15 mm of lead at each end and, in the middle, some black paint or soil. Brookman and Langdon, who have always made good Cumberland lead pencils, have become universally known. Despite all this, these pencils have a significant defect, which comes from the fact that the pieces of lead are not very large. They are cut into small, very thin slices that break when they are resawed or glued. So they introduce lengths of 7–8 cm (2–3 in.) into a pencil and glue another piece end to end to obtain the desired length. The glue used in this method of joining forms rock-hard parts, which are very inconvenient for the draftsman, whose work they can damage. Only later, another type of Spanish graphite was discovered and has been to this day.

Towards the end of the last century, Conté à Paris invented and obtained a patent for the manufacture of pencils using graphite from Spain (Malaga) or Germany combined with clay. This process has been adopted everywhere. The graphite mined from Malaga is in hard pieces and difficult to crush, so we mainly use the ones from Bohemia or Passau, Bavaria. It has also been found in France, especially in Rodez. Mr. Ch. Rolland discovered an excellent quality graphite on his land, but it must be prepared differently, and the manufacturers, who are accustomed to the old way, are not looking for another method.

§ I. Production

Take some German graphite, put it into a barrel; pour water on it, in a large enough quantity, to wash it, stir it, and let it settle for some time, at the end of which the lightweight particles that are not settled as quickly and remain in suspension are decanted through a very fine sieve, and poured into another tub. It is left for 12 hours, and the water is removed and poured into the first barrel. The sediment is washed into the other barrel, and a portion of the material is available for manufacture. This washing operation is repeated until there is no more fine material in the first barrel, so it is left to settle, removed from the barrel, put on a filter to drain, and finally dried. The residue of the first barrel, which can still be washed, is used to make ordinary pencils.

The composition of the pencils is primarily clay. Their quality depends much on the nature of this clay. Some types of clay are better than others; for this purpose, blue and greasy clay is usually used. Then, the manufacturer tries it out before deciding on the amount he needs to add. When this clay is left in the fire for a few hours, it must come out white and firm without being stone-like.

One must also be careful to obtain good graphite, which is pure, without any other admixture. There are places that do a great deal of trade in the lead pencil and mix it with pulverized slate or rubble. The main trade in this substance is in Regensburg (Bavaria). It must be obtained from a decent company there.

Good graphite should be shiny, light, and soapy to the touch, not too gray. It should come apart in water, not precipitate too quickly, yet not float too long. In the latter case, it would be mixed with clay or greasy earth.

The Spanish one is very good, even preferable to the German one, but it must be pulverized into an almost impalpable powder. When these two ingredients—graphite and clay—are washed, they must be kept—whether dry or not dry—in barrels or covered crates so that no dust or other foreign matter can get into them.

When preparing the graphite for pencils, mix it with the clay in a bucket or large container. They are ground together in a mill—either a cylinder mill or any other device ordinarily used to grind colors. This grinding is repeated several times so that the two materials are well mixed and perfectly ground; the more carefully this grinding is done, the better the quality of the pencils.

Four kinds of fine pencils are usually made. № 1 soft, № 2 less soft, № 3 hard, № 4 harder. The first types are used for artistic drawing, and the others for linear drawing, for offices, etc. There are two proportions combinations, and more clay is introduced to add hardness.

			Washed graphite		Washed clay	
A.	Nos.	1	5	parts	1	part
		2	4	—	1¼	—
		3	3	—	1	—
		4	2	—	1½	—

	Graphite				Clay
B. Nos. 1	6	parts	. . . .	1	part
2	5	—	. . . .	1	—
3 & 4	4	—	. . . .	1	—

The lead is prepared—after it has been drawn and baked—by taking white wax, or stearin, and dipping it in the manner indicated below.

For ordinary pencils, use half graphite and half clay; for inferior kinds, more well-washed clay.

When the materials are thoroughly ground, they are placed on boards to dry, and when they are almost dry, they are stacked so that they do not dry out completely. A portion of them is placed on a large stone built into a wall at the height of 80 cm (2½ ft.), surrounded by planks so that the pieces do not fall off, and they are beaten with a rounded piece of hardwood. This beating continues until they are tightly compressed, then they are shaped into rounded balls so they can be put into the spinning press.

§ II. Description of the Extrusion Machine

It is a small copper pipe, 12–15 mm thick, 45–50 cm (15–20 in.) long, and 8–10 cm (3–4 in.) in diameter. This barrel must be fixed on a very strong table in a very solid way. At one end, there is an opening into which a screen, made of copper 3–4 mm thick, pierced with small holes, and another spare nut, in the middle of which is a tube 2½ cm (1 in.) long and made of strong copper, covered with a cap nut, which in the middle has an opening of 5–6 mm. The other end of this press is also fixed in a very solid way on the table. A pressure screw carrying at the other end a piston of sole leather, supported by two iron plates, which enters exactly into the press at the other end of the pressure screw, is provided with a revolving spindle to make it work.

When the lead has been kneaded, the barrel is filled with it. The front opening is closed with the sieve nut, and the screw is turned so that the piston moves forward and the lead comes out in a thread through the sieve, like vermicelli. This kneading of the lead makes it more homogeneous, so it is repeated several times, after which it is reworked and reshaped into round sticks so that it can be rolled into the cylinder, which is closed with the cap nut, plugging the opening in the small nut that forms the cap. The lead inside is then squeezed with the piston to ensure it is dense enough not to leave a gap and is left for one to two hours, after which the cap is removed to remove what was used to plug the hole, and a copper or steel disc is placed in the middle, 4 mm thick, with a small opening in the middle, square, round, large or small, depending on the shape or size of the lead to be made.

On the table where the barrel is affixed, a plain wooden board 80 cm (2½ ft.) long and 32 cm (1 ft.) wide, with a small ledge at the back and exactly of height so that the pencil rests well straight on it while coming out of the pressing (barrel). Then, one workman takes hold of the winder, another is placed in front of the table, the winder is immediately turned, and the lead goes out through the small opening of the cap in thin threads, while the workman placed in front of the table guides it to the other end of the board. As soon as the person turning sees that it has reached the end, he stops. The lead thread is broken off, close to the cap's opening, and placed straight on the board. We continue this way, and when we have 8, 10, 12 threads, we gently push them to the small rim of the board with a ruler so that they remain straight. The entire board is loaded this way, and then the lead is evened out at each end; it is covered with small wooden planks, and a rail is also placed on the front so that it does not shift and is left until it is almost dry. These threads are then cut to the pencils' length and left to dry completely.

§ III. Cooking the Leads

You must have a brick stove, which draws well with a chimney at the top so that the draft is uniform. It will give an even fire through-out. This furnace should be (measured inside) 40–42 cm (15–16 in.) square, have an iron door at the top for the crucibles and coal, and a lower door for the ash pan. It should have two tiers of iron bars—one immediately above the coals and the other 16 cm (6 in.) higher. The oven must be arranged so that the crucibles can be surrounded by fuel and heated evenly.

The cylindrical crucibles are made of cast iron and measure 20–22 cm (9–10 in.) high and 7 cm (3 in.) in diameter. Each has a cast iron lid; They are filled with the lead. A little dry crushed sandstone is put in beforehand, and the lead is placed upright in the sandstone. The crucible is tilted a little so that when it is filled, sand or crushed sandstone can be added more easily so that it can be completely filled without any voids. It is capped with its cover, which is lined with moistened clay or wet soil.

The fire is prepared with charcoal, and two or three crucibles are placed on the first row of iron bars, covered with charcoal, and other crucibles are placed on the second row of iron bars, then the fire is lit so that it burns evenly, and the crucibles glow red evenly. The fire is maintained for at least four hours of red heat, after which it is left to die down until it is cold. Manufacturers who do not need a lot of lead can also cook in a fireplace over an iron grate. When the process is complete, the crucibles are removed, and when they are completely cool, they are opened to remove the lead from the sandstone and the dust. The lead that has been made according to process A is good to use, while the lead made according to process B receives the following handling:

A copper or iron pot of about 7–8 cm (9–10 in.) square is used. For this boiler, there are five screens made of wire cloth with meshes of 3–4 mm in size, attached by iron rods, which can be hooked by clamps in the top of the boiler so that they can be removed and put back easily.

The boiler is put on the fire, always over charcoal and not wood, because there is too much hazard from the flame. Add 1 kg to 1½ (2–3 lb.) of white wax or stearin (since stearin is cheaply available, it is preferred as a cheaper alternative). Melt until it is brought to the highest possible temperature. During the time that this material heats up, the cooked lead is placed on the wire mesh, about the contents of one to two large ones. When the stearin is boiling, the wire mesh is immersed with the lead. № 1 is left for one minute, № 2 for five minutes, № 3 for eight minutes, and № 4 for twelve to fifteen minutes. Remove, let drain, and place on paper to cool. When a grate has been removed, wait until the material becomes very hot again. It is also necessary to have another pot, or metal vessel, containing turpentine, which does not need to be on the fire, and as soon as the lead, especially № 3 and № 4, has been left to drip a little. It is immersed in the turpentine while it is still hot, long enough to dissolve any stearin or wax that may still be adhering, and finally, it is placed in a drying oven to evaporate the turpentine.

We usually make № 1 large, № 2 smaller, № 3 small, № 4 smaller. When it is very small, it can be left for a few minutes less in the primer. Always have a metal lid next to the pot on the fire that closes tightly, and in case the material catches fire, cover it with the lid to extinguish the flame. When the lead is cold and you see that it is still greasy, you clean it with a cloth. This lead is used for the superior pencils.

§ IV. Wood Assembly

Boards of cedar or linden wood are cut. For the square lead, one of these boards is thicker and the other thinner, calculating so that when the pencils are rounded, the lead is exactly in the middle. For the round lead, the two boards must be of equal thickness. After having the wood sawn into thin boards by a mechanical sawmill, it is cut into small planks.

The boards are cut to a length a few millimeters longer than the pencils and then cut with a circular saw, on the shaft of which there is also a cutter the size of the lead to be glued. This is how the small rods are cut, and the groove is made at the same time. This groove must be exactly in the middle, and when you take a cover made of thin board, these two pieces must form an edge. The table of this mechanism for the milling cutter must be established in such a way that it can be raised or lowered at will in order to adjust this milling cutter according to the groove to be made, and it is the same for the guide so that it can be advanced and retreated and at the same time adjust the distance that is left between the saw and the milling cutter by means of washers, in order to have the exact middle.

When all the wood is cut and grooved, the lead is introduced into the groove. To do this, the lead is taken in hand in order to be able to handle it comfortably, and it is placed in the grooves. Once this work is done, the lead is glued with strong glue, and for this purpose, three or four grooved rods are taken in one hand, glue is brushed into them, or the lead is introduced, as many covers are taken immediately afterward, they are coated with glue over them, and the grooves are covered. One puts the ones on the others well equally, and one repeats this gluing until one has glued 20–25 of them, which one puts in press. Then, secure them with a strap so they can not move, tighten them, and let them dry.

The press can hold 20 to 25 pencils side by side and is made of wood or iron, with two rods for feeding and covering the pencils, one at each end, about 2 to 3 cm (1 in.) from the end. On the front are two pressure screws for tightening. Care must be taken not to put too much glue all around to be able to soak it in, and if you see you've put too much on, remove it with a wet sponge. Leave in the press until the glue is dry, then separate the pencils and expose them to the air to complete the drying process. Saw them 4 mm longer than the desired finished length, then round them off with a plane or mandrel.

The planer is 18–20 cm (6–8 in.) long and 36 mm wide, with a copper base and a hole half the diameter of the pencils, and it moves in a runner very precisely. In the middle of this slide is an opening of 15 mm, and in the center is a rocker of the length of the pencils. At the top of this rocker, there is a pad closed at the top end, carrying a small steel rod with 3 small points on the side of the rocker. At the bottom is another pad divided in half. This pad is 40 mm long and covers a notch of the steel rod, whose end on the side of the rocker is also provided with three points, placed on the other end of the slide, a pad which is retained by a round opening, made in an iron plate. A spring pushes it against the pencils to retain them; at the end is attached an iron handle with a crosspiece. The rocker is made of wood, with a copper post of a width suitable to enter in the middle of the opening of the slide, with a screw of return adapted to fix the board, which enables the rocker to raise or lower it at will. In the middle of the upright is a **V**-shaped recess to put the pencil, which is supported by a corner of the entire slide length, which is about 80 cm (2½ ft.). This wedge binds it so that it cannot fall, with a return screw, to fix the pressure it must give. Once fixed, it remains invariably at the same height. To round it off, we take the small crosspiece in the left hand and pull it back, with the right hand a pencil that we put in support of the rocker. The spring pushes back the steel wire attached to it, and the pencil is clamped between two points. Then, one gives him some blows with the plane, and one cuts down an angle. As soon as this corner is cut, the wedge is removed, and the rocker falls. The pencil is turned with the crosspiece on the side that is already removed. The wedge is pushed back to put the support in its place. The next corner is cut, and then the other two corners. The pencil is now well-rounded; only a few strokes of the plane are needed to level it. You have to adjust the holder so that all the pencils are the same size.

Here is another way to round the pencils:

On a lathe bed, a headstock with a width of 10 cm (4 in.) is placed, with a hollow shaft. This shaft has a screw on it, like ordinary lathe shafts; on this screw is fixed a copper chuck of 28–30 mm, with an opening on the side, like a plane, to let the shavings out: there is placed an iron or chisel. The chuck is pierced with a hole that is slanted, the size of the pencil at the beginning of the size of the square pencil, and on the back side, the size of the rounded pencil. Then, the chisel must follow at this distance 14–15 mm in its pose. In front of this chuck is fixed a piece of iron with a square hole the size of the pencil. This shaft is moved with a lathe wheel and a pedal or with a large wheel of 1.8–2 m (5–6 ft.), which a workman turns. When it is in action, one places a pencil in the square of the guide, pushes it until it comes out from behind, then takes it in a pair of pliers with the left hand and pulls it gently until it is completely out. This is the easiest and quickest way, but great care must be taken to ensure that the iron (chisel) is sharp, the pencils are well glued, and the wood is of perfect quality.

When the pencils are rounded and also sawn to length, they are still rough at the end, so they must be trimmed so that the wood and leads are clean and shiny.

For this purpose, we have a trimming press, which consists of two strong wooden boards with iron on the top and bottom edges. These two boards fit exactly together and are the height of the pencils. They are provided with 100–150 round holes at all heights. These pencils must be exactly the size of the holes and a little longer than the length they should be after they are cut. These two boards are placed upright between two screws on a plain, straight board; on this latter board is fitted a ruler 2½ cm (1 in.) wide and 2 mm thick, running in a slide, precisely below the holes in the press. Then, we put a pencil in each hole until all are full, or equalize at the top by pressing so that all the pencils rest on the ruler; remove the ruler, and the pencils go down on the table and come out on both sides of the press, enough to have something to cut. We have a plane whose iron is laid flat and at an angle, with which we trim the ends; we give a few blows, and when the first side is finished, we turn the press, we put the ruler back so that the pencil cannot go down, and we trim the second.

Uneven pencils that cannot be trimmed with the press are trimmed with a knife that is 8 cm (3 in.) long and has a bevel on the right side and the other side flat. The pencils are trimmed by placing one end on a piece of white boxwood and cut into thin slices, after which they are polished with a polisher that has a cavity, or they are varnished with shellac and a buffer in the same way that cabinetmakers varnish furniture. For this, it is necessary to smooth it with sandpaper and to place the pencils on a board with many. This board has, at the top, bottom, and one side, a small edge so that the pencils do not fall; one takes the buffer with the right hand, and one turns the pencils with the left hand, after which they are stamped with the brand, and packed in dozens.

For each size pencil, you need a separate plane, support or a chuck, and a trimming press.

Writing Quills, Paste Glue and Drying Varnish

§ I. Writing Quills

In the earlier centuries, pens were mainly prepared in Holland or Hamburg: the former were transparent, and the latter were matte white. But later, the factories greatly multiplied, and today, we find them in every country.

The preparation of the feathers is a very simple operation and consists of soaking the feathers and then cooking them.

To make the Hamburg feathers and the transparent ones, you need a cast iron or wrought iron stove, 32–40 cm (12–15 in.) square, with a door at the top for feeding coal. This stove rests in a tub with a diameter of 1.2–1.5 m (4–5 ft.), full of sand, which is not too fine. There should be enough space between the sand and the stove grate so that a handful of feathers can be introduced. The furnace heats the sand until it becomes shiny.

The feathers from each side, or each wing, are sorted and put in two piles—one pile for feathers from the left wing and a separate pile for those from the right wing. For the so-called *Hamburg* white feathers, make bundles of five hundred feathers and put them in a damp place twelve hours before preparing them. For this, stir the sand with a small iron shovel to equalize and distribute the heat. An iron plate is attached to the right side of the knee, which is rounded to fit over the thigh and covered with leather; in the right hand, a strong knife without a cutting edge is held and heated in the sand. In the left hand, one takes five or six feathers, and more if one is well skilled, from the piles. Plunge them into the scorching sand: these feathers become then soft, and in this state, one moves them on the leather on the knee and rests them so that they are on the back, after which, with the hot knife which one took in hand, and with the point, pressing strongly on the top of the pipe, one brings back on the front while drawing so that the tail of the feather goes down to the point. It is detached at the same time from the hairs which are around the feather. The feathers are dipped again in the hot sand, scraped with the knife and put aside to cool. When they are cold, scrape the barb next to the tube again with a knife or a piece of glass.

The Dutch feathers are also sorted, and the right and left sides are separated. Use large boxes 15–16 cm (5–6 in.) in height and of such a size that they can contain five to six thousand feathers. These boxes are filled with fine wet sand, in which handfuls plant the feathers and tightly packed, and they are pushed in the whole length of the shaft. They are left in this way for at least 36 hours, and then they are removed as they are cooked. They are removed from the sand and wrapped in a wet cloth, which is placed next to the stove. The sand is stirred as for the white feathers, and three to four handfuls of these wet feathers are placed on top. The first handful is removed from the fire, the skin around the feathers is scraped off with the knife, and they are passed through the fire once more so that they are completely transparent, but this must be done quickly; otherwise, the other plumes will burn. Those who are not yet experienced enough should treat only a handful at a time until they are skilled enough to take more. It is important to make sure that the sand is hot but not so hot that it burns the feathers. This work done, it is passed to another worker, who thoroughly cleans these feathers so that they are immaculate. Then, remove the nib with an iron wire, and for that, insert an iron wire by the point of the nib at the bottom and push it to the bottom; there, turn it to catch the end of the nib, which is pulled to the bottom. Cut down the barb of the top of the tube, and sort by size and by number.

These feathers are transparent and clear, like white glass; if you want them to be greenish, wet the sand with potash or alum water. If you want them to be yellowish, wet it with nitric acid diluted with water and containing five to six percent, i.e., twelve parts of water to 1 ½ of acid. Finally, put them in packages of 25 and then of 100.

The raw feathers are bought by weight in Germany. The largest trade is in Leipsick and in Frankfurt on the Oder. Hamburg and Bohemia also do a large trade, Poland and Russia supply the most significant part. In all countries, the summer feathers are the best and are worth more than the winter ones because the summer feathers are more mature and not so fat.

The feathers of Pomerania are sought after in Hamburg for the finishing of white quills, and the feathers from Veser and Ostefrise for the transparent ones. These two kinds are always more expensive, and the 10 loth ones from these countries are larger and longer than those of Russia or Poland at 11 loth. Prussian (Àltemark) feathers are better than those from Kœnisberg.

It is easy to distinguish summer feathers from winter feathers in that summer feathers are worn at the end of the plumage, and winter feathers are round. It is necessary to take care that the feathers do not have white spots on the shafts; these spots do not disappear while preparing.

Also, feathers are often bought that have not been weighed, and those unfamiliar with this are often deceived because the best ones have been removed, and to give the required weight, the wing tips have been inserted.

A wing has ten good feathers: the first is the wing tip, the other four are the best, and the next five are also good but light.

The manufacturers who prepare the feathers also establish their numbers by weight and distinguish the number by string color.

To make round packages of 25, one simply operates by hand. When one wants to put them in square packages, one has for each size a series of tin squares of 3 cm (1 in.) height; one takes 25 feathers by hand, one chooses five to put them behind, and the five best to put them in front. One then fills the tin square, and one binds with the string of the desired color, forming a square package.

§ II. Manufacture of a Very Good and Cheap Paste Glue

This glue is very good for bookbinders and highly suitable for weavers, etc. Grate half a kg (1 lb.) of potatoes and add three liters of river water, then boil while stirring for four to five minutes. Remove from the fire, and add little by little 16 grams (½ oz.) of finely powdered alum, constantly stirring until the glue is clear and transparent.

§ III. Drying Varnish for Bookbinders

Mix the following in a three-liter bottle:

Spirit of wine at 36° (97°F) 1	litre
Washed sandarac 325	gm
Washed mastic 65	—
Camphor 16	—
Venetian turpentine 65	—

Add some coarsely crushed glass to prevent the resins from sticking together.

In another bottle, 125 grams (4 oz.) of bitumen of Judea is placed in 385 grams (12 oz.) of oil of spike lavender or naphtha and left to melt in a water bath. When everything is melted, add the sandarac to the bottle containing the spirit of wine and put it in a water bath; cover the bottle with a piece of bladder, prick it a few times with a needle, and stir it occasionally. When everything is melted, let it rest and filter through felt. If the varnish is too strong, add some spirits of wine.

Colored Inks

№ 1. *Red A.* Take half a kg (1 lb.) of grated or chopped brazil-wood is boiled with 65 grams (2 oz.) of alum in four liters of vinegar for 15–20 minutes and left to stand for 3–4 days.

Red B. Take half a kg of brazilwood, 100 grams (3 oz.) of alum, 65 grams of cream of tartar, boiled in forty parts of filtered water. It is clarified, left to rest, and candy sugar is added.

№ 2. *Carmine.* Take 32 grams (1 oz.) of carmine № 40 and dilute it in water mixed with 125 grams (4 oz.) of cream of tartar. Then, stir in volatile alkali until the proper shade is obtained. Filter and strain with water until the ink is sufficiently clean, and finally, add candy sugar.

№ 3. *Blue.* Pulverize one part premium indigo. Put this in a glass vessel and pour four parts of 60° concentrated sulfuric acid over it. Let it stand for a day; then pour in, little by little, 4–5 liters of water, stirring well with a glass rod; then add as much powdered chalk as acid. Let it stand for 48 hours; clarify it and add gum arabic dissolved in water.

№ 4. *Yellow A.* Ten parts of Avignon berries, boiled with one part of alum in forty parts of filtered water; gum is then added.

Yellow B. Take two parts gamboge and one part alum; boil in 20–24 parts water, and filter.

№ 5. *Green.* Blue ink is mixed with yellow ink.

№ 6. *Violette.* Mix red and blue ink.

№ 7. *White.* Take bismuth oxide or silver white and grind it fine with strongly gummed water. This ink will settle; you must not make it too light. Stir it before writing.

№ 8. Black

Chopped brazilwood. 3   parts
Crushed walnuts (small, heavy nuts) 3   —
Calcined copperas 2   —
Cloves 51   gm
Sprinkle with a few handfuls of salt
to prevent fungus.

Boil 3–4 hours, let stand, and strain. The copperas is calcined by putting it in an iron pot on the fire until it is red.

№ 9. Blue Black

Crushed walnuts. 2   parts
Brazilwood 4   —
Calcined copperas 1   —
Cyprus vitriol 1   —
Cloves 51   gm
A few handfuls of salt

Boil 4–5 hours, filter and add gum.

№ 10. Copy Ink

Take black ink and add a larger amount of gum and white honey or candy sugar.

№ 11. Powdered Ink for Travelers

This reduced to a very fine powder.

Pomegranate rind, well-dried 3   parts
Calcined copperas 1   —

Each substance is ground separately and then mixed. This powder must be kept in tin cans because it will melt in the air. When you want to write, mix a pinch of it in water or beer, and you get very good ink.

Pastels

§ I. The Base for Pastels

Pastels are solid, chalky colors molded into crayons.

The base color of all pastels is white chalk, namely Meudon white, Spanish white, bone ash, calcined alabaster powder, or white pipe clay. All these materials must be thoroughly washed and cleaned of any iron impurities they may contain.

In the past, the best pastels were made in Lausanne, Switzerland, but the manufacturer who made them did not reveal his process. We, therefore, tried to imitate his products, and we presume that their quality came from the white he used. After long research, we finally made very good pastels, and with the help of practice and experience, we were able to surpass the Swiss pastels. Especially in terms of color, these products have been perfected.

All colors must be ground very finely—either with water or dry—and reduced to a pure powder.

In general, colors made with acids, such as lakes, Prussian blue, indigo, etc., cannot be ground with water because they are already rather hard, and by grinding them with water, they would become even harder. They must be reduced to an immensely fine powder by grinding and mixed with the white.

Never use metallic oxide whites, such as lead white, zinc white, or bismuth white, which blacken easily due to the fumes of sulfur.

In pastel painting, a great variety of colors are needed, and in each color, an endless number of gradated shades. Each color is made in 5, 6, 7, or even more shades, from the darkest to the lightest.

There are several binders, such as milk, barley decoction, gum tragacanth, and wax soap, which must be used in the manner indicated in the formula for each color.

The color should be ground on a very hard marble and with a millstone of the same quality. The powdered color is mixed with white, and the water is allowed to evaporate by exposing it to air and sunlight and always covering it with paper until the material is dry enough to be molded into crayons. Many manufacturers put it between sheets of unsized paper, applying pressure to extract the moisture, but in the process, they remove the binder.

The best way to form pastels is to roll the mixture between the hands to make crayons. Take a hazelnut-sized amount of the material and roll it between the hands until the length is 7–8 cm. (2½–3 in.). Then, roll it on a table with a small wooden board of a width of 7–8 cm. (2½–3 in.) until the pastels are precisely the width of the board so that all are of equal length. They are then placed on boards to dry and rubbed with fine sandpaper to give them a bit of smoothness and a better appearance.

Three kinds of pastels are made: soft pastels, semi-hard pastels, and hard pastels. The latter are usually wrapped with colored paper or Italian straw. A point of about 2 cm (1 in.) is made, and the rest is wrapped with paper or straw rolled around it and glued with gum. They are packaged in boxes of a dozen or two. These last pastels are usually made only for children and in fewer shades; twenty to twenty-four are enough.

Avoid, as much as possible, using Vandyke brown, natural umber, bistre, or any other colors that are already greasy, brittle, or crumbly before being ground, and replace them with a mixture of various other colors, as indicated.

§ II. Preparation of the Wax & Soap Mixture

Take half a kg (1 lb.) of white Marseilles soap. Cut it into small pieces, and soak them for 24 hours in five liters of river water. Then, put them on the fire in an earthenware pot, and when all of the soap has melted, add 1 kg (2 lb.) of white wax. Stir until the wax is well melted.

§ III. Gum Tragacanth

Leave one part gum tragacanth—as white as possible—to soak for several days in twelve parts water; then pass it through a sieve.

§ IV. Barley

Soak one part of barley in six parts of water for several days or put on the fire and let it boil until the barley begins to swell and split. Pass it through a sieve or cloth; the liquid is used.

§ V. Milk

The milk must always be fresh and pure. I prefer not to use it because it is not always of high quality and sours too readily; the barley decoction is therefore preferable.

§ VI. Colors

The colors and the white are quite thickly ground with water. When everything has been ground and mixed for the shades, add the binder; mix using your hands so that the dough is well homogenized.

№ 1. Vermilion Red

Vermilion		Bone ash	
6	parts	1	parts
5	—	2	—
4	—	3	—
3	—	4	—
2	—	5	—
1	—	6	—
½	—	7	—
¼	—	7	—

Bind with white pipe clay and very little gum.

№ 2. Orange Lead

Same proportion as for vermilion, but instead of bone ash, use Spanish white and more pipe clay with little soap.

№ 3. Red Brown

Red brown		Spanish white crushed w/water	
6	parts	2	parts
5	—	3	—
4	—	4	—
3	—	5	—
2	—	6	—

Bind with pipe clay and soap.

№ 4. Red Brown

Iron oxide (colcothar)		Bone ash ground with water	
6	parts	3	parts
5	—	4	—
4	—	5	—
3	—	6	—
2	—	7	—
1	—	9	—
1	—	12	—

Not much pipe clay, and more wax soap.

There are several shades of iron oxide, and this color is very consistent and very suitable for use.

№ 5. Red Lake

Wood that we grind		Bone ash ground into a fine, soft powder	
6	parts	1	parts
5	—	2	—
4	—	3	—
3	—	4	—
2	—	5	—

Bind with barley decoction.

№ 6. Carmine Red

Crushed carmine № 40		Bone ash	
6	parts	2	parts
4	—	4	—
2	—	6	—

Bind with barley and a little pipe clay.

№ 7. Carmine Red Lake

Crushed carmine lake		Bone ash	
6	parts	1	parts
5	—	2	—
4	—	3	—
3	—	4	—
2	—	5	—
1	—	6	—
½	—	7	—

Bind with barley and pipe clay.

Use a very high-quality carmine lake, which has a very nice shade and is soft to the touch. It is better to choose the one that exists in the trade under the name of English lake.

№ 8. Madder

Madder Crushed into extra-fine powder		Bone ash	
6	parts	2	parts
4	—	4	—
2	—	6	—
1	—	8	—
½	—	8	—

Bind with barley decoction and a little pipe clay.

№ 9. Brown (imitation Cassel Earth/Vandyke brown)

Iron oxide (colcothar) of a beautiful shade 4   parts

Vine black 2   —

Ochre from Rhue 1   —

Caput mortuum (Vandyke brown) 1   —

Grind these colors together and take:

From the mixture above		Spanish white	
6	parts	2	parts
5	—	3	—
4	—	4	—
3	—	5	—
2	—	6	—

Bind with sufficient pipe clay and little gum tragacanth.

All shades of brown can be obtained by adding more or less iron oxide, yellow, or black. One can also use Berlin blue and allow it to redden over an open fire in a crucible, and mix it after grinding it to powder; but then one must add more Vandyke brown and take care that it is genuine and not too purplish, for all sorts of browns are often sold in place of this color, regardless of how cheap it is.

№ 10. Yellow

A. Ochre from Rhue Ground with Water

Ochre from Rhue		Spanish white	
6	parts	2	parts
5	—	3	—
4	—	4	—
3	—	6	—
2	—	8	—

Bind with pipe clay and pure wax soap.

B. Ochre from Rhue Ground with Water

Ochre from Rhue		Iron oxide (colcotar)		Spanish white	
4	parts	2	parts	3	parts
3	—	1½	—	4	—
2	—	1	—	5	—
1	—	½	—	6	—
½	—	¼	—	7	—

Bind with pipe clay and a little wax soap.

Different shades can be made from this yellow. To obtain the Italian yellow, add a very little vine black. For other colors, add more or less ochre or iron oxide, Vandyke brown or calcined Berlin blue.

№ 11. Chrome Yellow

Light or dark. You can find all shades in the trade; it is preferable to choose Sponer's.

Chrome yellow		Bone ash	
6	parts	3	parts
5	—	4	—
4	—	5	—
3	—	6	—
2	—	7	—
1	—	8	—
½	—	9	—

Bind with pipe clay and a little wax soap.

You can create different tones by adding a bit of orange lead or vermilion.

№ 12. Naples Yellow

Genuine Naples yellow is not suitable for making pastels because of its metallic composition, which darkens easily under the influence of the antimony sulfide it contains. It should be imitated with pale chrome yellow, mixed with half royal yellow or orpiment, and mixed with bone ash. One can obtain yellows of different shades—mineral, Indian, etc.—by adding a little orange lead.

An orange is produced by adding half orange lead or vermilion and bone ash mixed with pipe clay and soap.

№ 13. Blue

Indigo blue or Berlin blue is always hard, so care must be taken to make a paste that has the consistency needed for molding and not apply too much pressure.

Only one shade is easily made by mixing one or two parts of bone ash with six parts of powdered Prussian blue and adding a little barley decoction. For the other tones, use mineral blue.

Mineral blue		Bone ash	
6	parts	1	parts
5	—	2	—
4	—	3	—
3	—	4	—

Mineral blue		Bone ash	
2	parts	5	parts
1	—	6	—

Bind with barley decoction and a little pipe clay.

The mineral blue must be a lovely color, pure and light. It is best to get it from the Milori factory.

Mineral blue crushed with water		Bone ash	
6	parts	1	parts
5	—	2	—
4	—	3	—
3	—	4	—
2	—	5	—
1	—	6	—
1	—	8	—

Bind with pipe clay and soap and very little gum tragacanth.

№ 14. Nice Cobalt Blue and Ultramarine

Same proportions as above, but crushed longer. Cobalt blue can be imitated by using ultramarine and adding more white and very little carmine, or madder lake.

№ 15. Blue Black

Add some vine black and white to the mineral blue in the same proportion.

№ 16. Extra Fine Violet

Ultramarine		Carmine		Spanish white	
1	parts	1	parts	1	parts
1	—	1	—	2	—
1	—	1	—	3	—
1	—	1	—	4	—
1	—	1	—	5	—

Bind with pipe clay and a little wax soap.

You can get shades that are redder or bluer by including more or less carmine and more or less blue. By adding more white, we obtain lilac.

№ 17. Green
Grind with water:

Milori green		Bone ash	
6	parts	2	parts
5	—	3	—
4	—	4	—
3	—	5	—
2	—	6	—
1	—	7	—

Bind with pipe clay and soap.

This color is a beautiful natural green: to make a green-blue, add mineral blue, and for a more yellow tone, add some pale chrome yellow.

If one does not have Milori green, use a good Prussian blue that is not too hard. Crush and reduce it to powder. Boil one part blue pigment with two parts of alum; put it in a large container and pour water into it. Decant and add fresh water when all the color is settled at the bottom. Repeat this operation until the blue color has no more alum taste, then mix it with pale chrome yellow (canary color) to the desired hue.

№ 18. Green Black

Vine black		Pale chrome yellow		Spanish white	
5	parts	1	parts	2	parts
4	—	2	—	3	—
3	—	3	—	4	—
2	—	4	—	5	—
1	—	5	—	6	—
1	—	6	—	8	—
½	—	7	—	9	—

Bind with pipe clay and soap.

№ 19. Green Brown

Vine black		Chrome yellow		Iron oxide		Spanish white	
4	parts	2	parts	2	parts	2	parts
3	—	3	—	3	—	3	—
2	—	3	—	4	—	4	—
2	—	3	—	5	—	5	—
1	—	3	—	6	—	6	—

You can make darker shades by adding black, yellow, iron oxide, or white. Bind with pipe clay and soap.

№ 20. Bistre

Use two parts lampblack, two parts vine black, two parts iron oxide, and two parts white; bind with pipe clay and soap. By adding Spanish white, you can make gradations to the gray tone.

№ 21. White

Bone ash, bound strongly with pipe clay and soap. A small amount of ultramarine can be added to make a milk-white tone.

№ 22. Flesh Color

Use two parts ochre from Rhue, one part yellow chrome, half a part iron oxide, and five parts bone ash crushed with water. Or make the shades by adding white and bone ash for nine to ten shades. Bind with pipe clay and soap; grind with water.

№ 23. More Pinkish Flesh Color

Use iron oxide and orange lead. Use white to make lighter shades.

№ 24. Black

Use three parts of calcined lampblack, three parts of vine black and one part of white. Shades are mixed with the white until almost blue, and are bound with pipe clay and soap. It is necessary to grind the lampblack with water mixed with spirits of wine. It is preferable to use a calcined lampblack.

№ 25. Darker Black

Use five parts German or Paris lampblack crushed with water and finely ground, with two parts dry white pipe clay and one part Prussian blue. Pastels are molded, and when they are very dry, they are enclosed in a well-sealed iron box, and exposed to the fire, where they are held for one hour at red heat; they are allowed to cool before being removed from the box. These pastels are matte and velvety black. They can be made more or less hard by adding pipe clay. It is better to mix the lampblack with spirit of wine diluted with water to grind it more easily.

One can make all the shades and hues by mixing the colors; to obtain the shades, take a little color on a piece of glass, add white and dilute it by mixing with a small brush; then makes a few thick lines on paper and let it dry.

§ VII. General Rules

In the manufacture of pastels, it is necessary to take the best quality colors—pure and without any admixture—and to have pure bone ash. Manufacturers often calcine all sorts of materials with bones, which also become white when calcined. Besides, this operation is easy, and one can calcine very well oneself.

Bones from cooked meat are cleaned and dried. They are placed in a fireplace, covered with hot coals, and the fire is kept going until they turn white; they are pulverized and ground into a very fine powder.

Pulverized alabaster can be used, but it is better to do without it because it is very absorbent and harder.

Avoid using too much wax soap because it would make the pastel too greasy, and it must be very liquid when used.

Semi-hard pastels are made in the same proportions as soft pastels. Only more white pipe clay is added, and a little soap.

For firm or hard pastels, more pipe clay is used, and a little traga-canth is added. If too much is used, they will not mark.

The pastels are usually put in flat or double-bottomed boxes of 160 to 170. The empty space is filled with bran and covered with cotton.

1	box contains around	130	to	140
½	—	60	to	65
¼	—	30	to	33

The number is never fixed because pastels are not of equal size. Some colors have more shrinkage than others.

Various Fabrications

§ I. Preparation of Gold and Silver for Painting

Fine gold leaf is obtained from the goldbeater and milled into a fine powder with honey on a slab. It is repeatedly washed with hot water and mixed with egg white or gum water.

For silver, silver leaf is used, and the process is the same as for gold.

§ II. Tinder Paper

The invention of chemical matches has considerably reduced the consumption of tinder everywhere, but in certain regions, the use of tinder persists, and there is still some profit in making tinder paper, especially when all sorts of printed papers can be used.

To make this tinder paper, boil 250 grams (8 oz.) of powdered litharge in four liters of wood vinegar[1] for a good hour. Remove the liquid from the fire and leave it to settle. Then, the liquid is decanted. Add as much clear water to the solution as it has lost in volume. Allow to cool. Soak old paper (without glue) in this liquid. Lay one sheet on top of the other and press lightly. Hang it on lines to dry; when this paper is dry, it will catch fire as easily as tinder.

§ III. Manufacture of Shoe Polish

It would be of great advantage to the paper trade and to the manufacturers of ink and sealing wax to deal with the manufacture of

---

1   *wood vinegar*—Pyroligneous acid

shoe polish. Because this process is simple and can be made in small quantities, we have thought it useful to introduce a description of its manufacture in this work.

Almost all shoe polish is, in most cases, composed of gum, sugar, lampblack or bone black, and sulfuric acid. These substances have the property of giving a beautiful luster to the leather, but because of the addition of sulfuric acid, they damage the leather and cause it to deteriorate. It is much more advantageous to make a shoe polish that gives the leather a beautiful shine and maintains it in a state of suppleness, but at the same time does not destroy it. These are the advantages and qualities that a good shoe polish must have, and we will give the method to make it.

A. Varnish for Patent Leather Shoes

Take four parts of Senegal gum [gum arabic], dissolve in sixteen parts of lukewarm water, crush the gum, pour it into the lukewarm water, and stir until all the gum is melted.

Then add four parts of lampblack, and stir to mix it all together.

To make lampblack for this purpose, fill an iron crucible or pot with lampblack, press it down firmly, cover it with an iron lid, and seal the joints with clay or stove earth. It is introduced into a fire and maintained for half an hour at a red heat; when the vessel is cooled, the quantity of black needed is taken and crushed with spirit of wine and added to the gum solution.

This varnish can be left in a liquid state or dried and made into tablets. By letting it dry halfway and forming, it can then be inserted into square or round tin molds, where it will dry completely.

The molds should be greased a little before putting the paste in so that the tablet will come out more easily.

When you want to use the varnish, just dilute it with a little water.

B. Cream Polish

To make this paste, which gives luster to the leather and keeps it supple, take four parts of fish glue and chop and cut it with a chisel to break it into small pieces. Put them in a vessel and add:

Brandy 8   parts
Water. 8   —

Put on a gentle fire, stirring often, until the glue is completely melted. It is then passed through a sieve and added:

White soap. 16   parts
River water 16   —

When this soap solution and the fish glue solution are mixed, let it boil for another fifteen minutes. At the same time, take:

Calcined lampblack 16   parts
Starch 16   —

Put it on the fire and let it reduce to half, then let it cool down. This wax can be used in this state or left to dry and pressed into tablets in tin molds, and then, when desired, it is diluted in a little water.

C. Cheap Shoe Polish—Almost as Good as the Last One

Strong glue 8   parts
White soap. 16   —

Everything is dissolved in a sufficient quantity of hot water and poured over:

Calcined lampblack 8   parts
Starch 8   —

The lampblack must be quenched in vinegar (diluted with water) or diluted brandy; a paste is made of the mixture. It can be kept as is or dried in tablets.

§ IV. Manufacture of Sandpaper and Emery Paper

Sandpaper

Ever since sandpaper replaced shark skin and *polissoirs*,[2] the demand for this type of paper has been so great that several manufacturers are dedicated solely to its preparation. Many families now earn their living from its production.

Five different types of sandpaper are made.

№   0. Very fine.

       1. Less fine.

       2. Coarser.

       3. Even coarser.

       4. Very coarse.

For each type of sandpaper, it is necessary to have a separate sieve similar to the one used by millers. The sieves are made of two rounds or discs of wood with a diameter of 30–40 cm (12–18 in.), attached by four (or sometimes five) slats measuring 70–80 cm (2–2½ ft.) in length. These slats must be tenoned around the perimeter in such a way that they do not protrude. Around this drum, one nails on two layers of canvas, using small, closely-placed brads so that nothing can pass between them. One sews the two edges of the fabric together very evenly and then covers the seam with a sewn ribbon.

At each end are fixed strong iron pins, 24–30 mm in diameter, of which the back one is 6–8 cm (2–3 in.) long and the front one twice as long. A perfectly fitted hatch on the front wooden dowel allows the crushed glass to be taken in and out.

This sifter must be enclosed in a box large enough to allow it to turn easily and that is deep enough to hold the emerging powder. This sifter is placed on supports at the front and back so that it cannot shift forward or backward. The front side of the box must be able to slide between two tracks so that it can be removed and the sifter can

2   Polissoir—tightly bound broom straw used to polish wood.

be taken out. The front iron pin must protrude out of the box so it can be attached to the crank used to turn the sifter.

Glass is crushed in an iron mortar and sifted with a sieve that does not allow more than № 4 to pass through. Sifter № 0 is filled halfway with this crushed glass, placed in its box, closed tightly, and rotated until nothing more passes through. Then, the fine powder is removed from the box. The crushed glass remaining in the sifter is taken out and then processed through sifter № 1. The process continues the same way until sifter № 4. The remaining glass must be taken to the mortar to be crushed again. In this way, one obtains five different sizes of glass particles and then properly stores them for use. This operation wears out the cloth very badly, so it is advantageous to use metallic cloth or mesh.

When you want to make sandpaper, proceed as follows: Melt one part of strong glue in four parts of water; when the glue is melted, use a brush to apply it to the paper and then immediately cover it with the glass powder. The paper is left to dry, and when it is completely dry, it is dry-brushed to remove the powder that is not attached to it.

The paper used to make ledgers is usually used for this purpose.

Emery Paper

Emery paper, which is used to polish metals, is made in much the same way. Fine emery is mixed with linseed oil varnish until it forms a light paste. This paste is applied to sheets of paper and left to dry. If the paper is not sufficiently covered, a second layer is applied. The paper is pressed when it is dry so that it is even and smooth.

§ V. Production of Rubber Cakes

It is not difficult to dissolve the rubber, and this can be done over an open fire with turpentine, asphalt oil, naphtha, or essential oil of tar derived from lamp oil. However, it is very difficult to restore it to its former state, as it takes a long time for the oil to evaporate. The material always retains a bad odor, and the tablets made with this rubber are never as good as natural rubber. In England, a much better process is followed, by means of which the rubber does not lose its original properties but becomes purer.

Rubber pieces are taken and immersed in hot water to soften them, washed thoroughly and cut into thin strips, which are then dropped into water, placed on the fire and boiled until they are softened. In this state, the rubber is passed between two rollers that can be heated to 30–40° [86–104°F] while always keeping them wet so that they do not stick. It is worked until the strips have become as thin as paper. This operation is advantageous because it fuses all the parts, which come out in very uniform thin sheets. In this state, it is put into molds and placed in a continuous pressure press or a hydraulic press, where it is left for 24 hours. The molds are greased with lard so that the rubber can easily be removed, and then it is cut into pieces.

Description of the Molds

Squares are made of strong iron, 16, 20, and 24 cm (8, 10, and 12 in.) square, 15–18 cm (6–8 in.) high, and well joined inside. The bottom must be fitted precisely and be removable. The cover is also fitted exactly, but in such a way that it can follow the mass of rubber, which descends with the pressure. When the mold is filled, the material is compressed by hand with a piece of iron pushing more material into the mold, and the cover is placed over it. This cover must be smooth and flat at the top, with a ring that penetrates the cover and leaves nothing protruding so that the pressure is evenly distributed. It must be very strong, and perhaps even one-third of the depth of the mold, because if the rubber is not forced into the mold, it will sink more than the cover can and leave gaps in it.

If you want to make a lot, you can use heavy presses where you can put several molds next to each other, so the molds and the lids must all be precisely the same height.

Hardwood boards can also be used at the beginning of the process when there is a danger that the rubber will sink lower than the lid and thus escape the pressure. One of these boards is placed on the cover, and when the rubber block is to be removed from the mold, it is placed on two strong iron rods, which are placed on both sides of the mold so as not to hinder the removal. It is covered under the lid with several of these boards, and it is subjected to the press. The rubber block is then hung in the air, but not under the sun or heat, for a few days to dry.

A copper strip is made of the same size as the rubber block but taller so that it can be placed on a wooden board that is fitted into the square one. Notches are made in this square board with a saw, which penetrates the wooden board. These are cut to the desired size, which is usually between 16 and 32 grams (½–1 oz.). Take a knife of double the length of the rubber block and 4–5 cm wide.

The notches in the copper square shall not be greater than the thickness of the knife, which must be very thin. Dip the knife in cold water and then saw down to the wooden board. When the whole board is cut, you will have other strips of copper, also bearing notches to cut it into smaller tablets, which are again put dry.

SPECIMENS

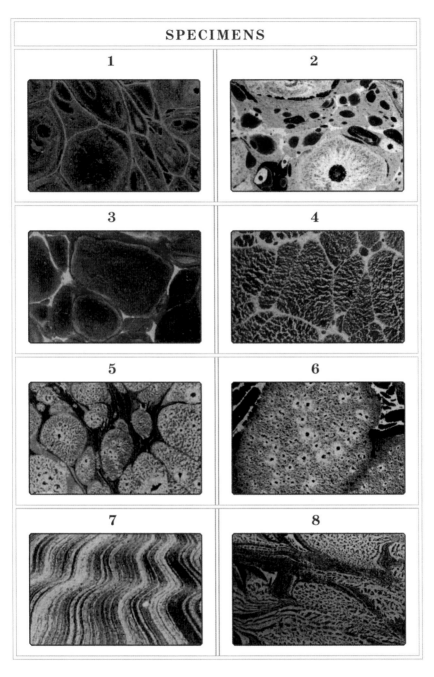

Images on the right were scanned from the publisher's copy and those on the left are from a copy held by the Bibliothèque National du France. The specimens in Fichtenberg's 1852 edition measure approximately 3.5 × 2 cm.

SPECIMENS   163

SPECIMENS

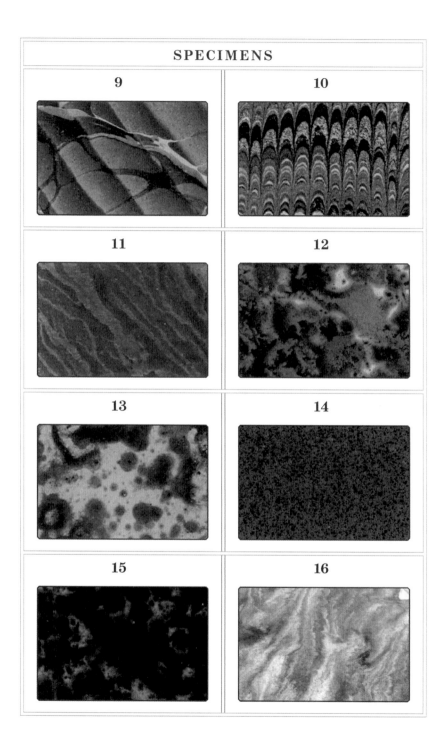

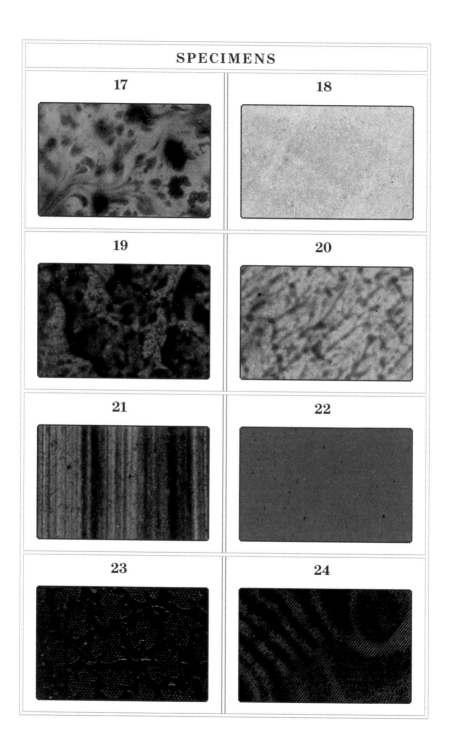

SPECIMENS

17   18

19   20

21   22

23   24

SPECIMENS

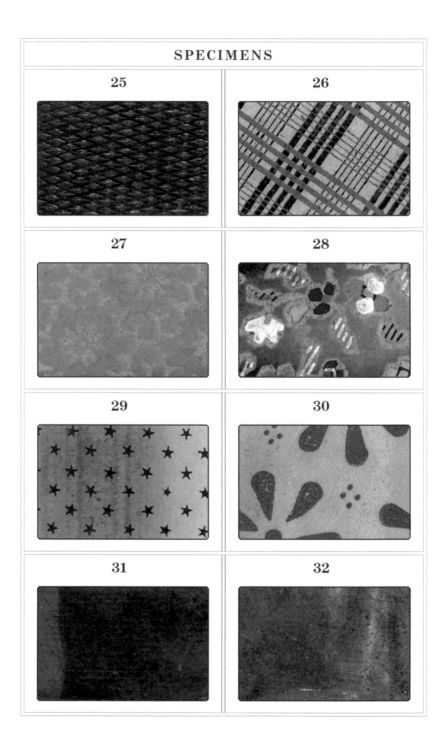

25

26

27

28

29

30

31

32

SUPPLEMENTAL MATERIAL

Recueil abrege des principales familles
17th-century French binding.
The British Library.

Fichtenberg's 1852 Edition

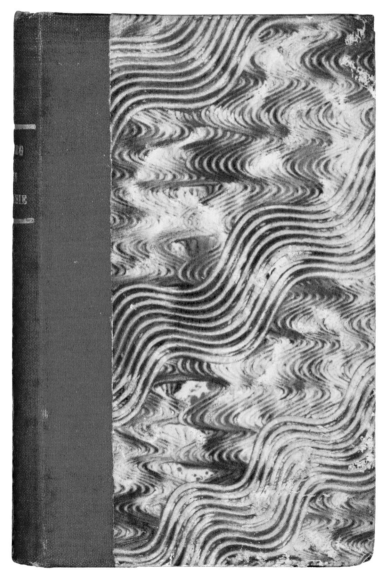

The publisher's copy, purchased from Llibres del Mirall of Barcelona, Spain, is bound in paste paper with red cloth. (Shown at actual size.)

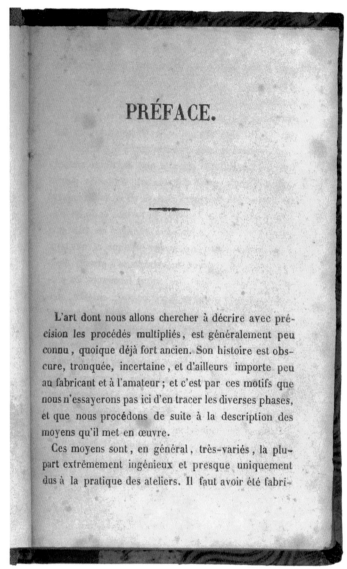

PRÉFACE.

L'art dont nous allons chercher à décrire avec précision les procédés multipliés, est généralement peu connu, quoique déjà fort ancien. Son histoire est obscure, tronquée, incertaine, et d'ailleurs importe peu au fabricant et à l'amateur ; et c'est par ces motifs que nous n'essayerons pas ici d'en tracer les diverses phases, et que nous procédons de suite à la description des moyens qu'il met en œuvre.

Ces moyens sont, en général, très-variés, la plupart extrêmement ingénieux et presque uniquement dus à la pratique des ateliers. Il faut avoir été fabri-

The 1852 edition was quite small. The first page of the Preface is shown above at actual size.

Comparison of Fichtenberg's Specimens from Different Copies

While the plan had been to use the specimens at the end of the publisher's copy of Fichtenberg's book, it was clear that could not be accomplished without damaging the book. The samples were simply too close to the binding to reveal the entire image when scanning. Since this was not an option, all of Fichtenberg's samples from the left-hand side of the page were replaced with those from copies that are available online.

The following table shows examples of the variations of the specimens that exist from copy to copy. [These are reproduced at approximately 73% of their original size.] The samples from the "publisher's copy," shown in the first column, are cut off due to the reasons stated above, but enough of each image remains to clearly illustrate these differences.

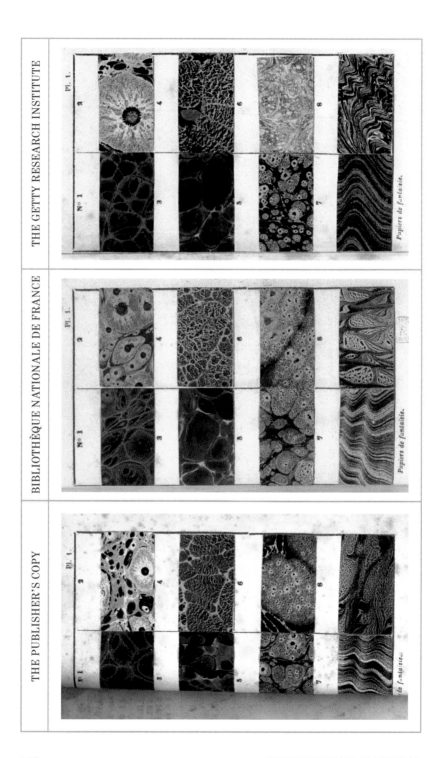

THE GETTY RESEARCH INSTITUTE

BIBLIOTHÈQUE NATIONALE DE FRANCE

THE PUBLISHER'S COPY

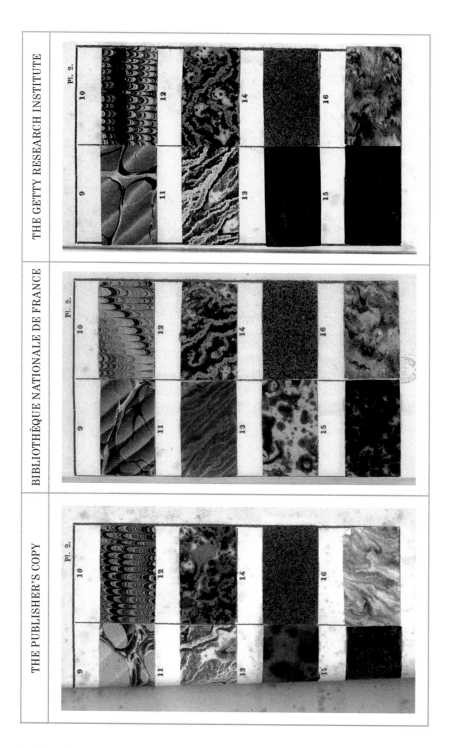

SPECIMENS FROM DIFFERENT COPIES 173

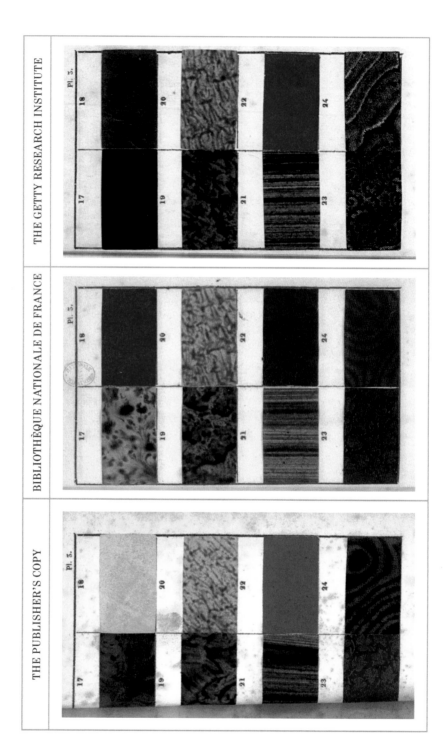

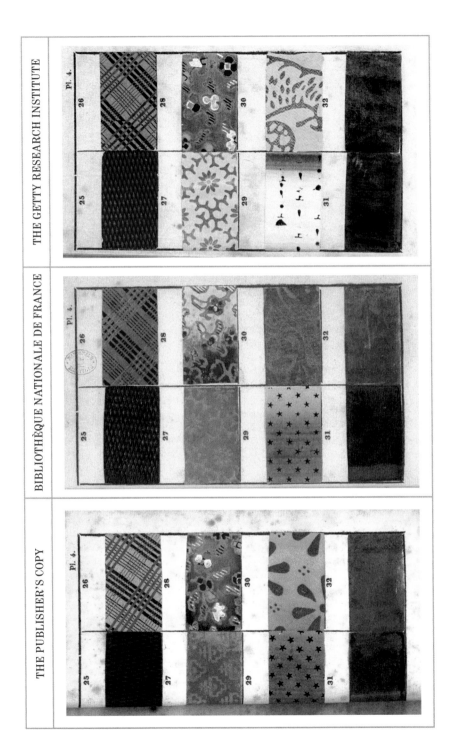

- THE GETTY RESEARCH INSTITUTE (Pl. 4, specimens 25–32)
- BIBLIOTHÈQUE NATIONALE DE FRANCE (Pl. 4, specimens 25–32)
- THE PUBLISHER'S COPY (Pl. 4, specimens 25–32)

Various Mentions of Fichtenberg

1783 SALOMON ASSER FICHTENBERG was born in Paderborn, Germany.[1] It's unclear when he emmigrated to France, but it, based on the other dates in this timeline, seems likely that it was between 1825 and 1827.

1820 FANNY FICHTENBERG was born to Salomon Asser Fichtenberg and Marthe Heumann in Cologne, Germany.[2]

1822 MAURICE FICHTENBERG was born to Salomon Asser Fichtenberg and Marthe Heumann in Cologne, Germany.[3]

1825 SOPHIE FICHTENBERG was born to Salomon Asser Fichtenberg and Marthe Heumann in Cologne, Germany.[4]

1827 [Patent issued] "To sirs Fichtenberg and Company, represented, in Paris, by sir SALOMON ASSER FICHTENBERG, at Mr. Albert's, rue Neuve-St.-Augustin, № 28, a 10-year importation and perfection patent, for chemical and manufacturing improvements in the manufacture of colored papers, imitating granite and various marbles, and in the means and processes of lustering, glazed or satin finishing them."[5]

1832 "MESSRS. FICHTENBERG & COMPAGNIE, *manufacturers of marbled papers and pencils, Paris, rue des Trois Bornes, № 26.*

1 Fichtenberg, Roger. *Journal d'un résistant juif dans le Sud-Ouest.* [*Diary of a Jewish Resistance fighter in the Southwest of France.*] Centre National Deu Livre. Paris. 2019. p. v.

2 According to information from the record of her 1899 death. *Paris, France, Births, Marriages, and Deaths, 1680–1930.* Archives de Paris, Paris, France. *Actes de naissance, de mariage et de décès.*

3 According to information from the record of his 1888 death. *Paris, France, Births, Marriages, and Deaths, 1680–1930.* Archives de Paris, Paris, France. *Actes de naissance, de mariage et de décès.*

4 According to information from the record of her 1876 death. *Paris, France, Births, Marriages, and Deaths, 1680–1930.* Archives de Paris, Paris, France. *Actes de naissance, de mariage et de décès.*

5 *Bulletin des sciences technologiques.* Vol. 3. 1827. p. 207.

"In addition to marbled papers, among which perfectly imitated granites were featured, these manufacturers presented a series of samples of pencils offering six degrees of hardness, according to the processes of Messrs. *Brockmann* and *Langden*, of London. Successful experiments on French iron carbide lead will enable these manufacturers to substitute it for the Spanish and German lead used to date."[6]

1834   "*Colors in tablets; pastel pencils; paintings imitating wood; safflower red; furniture polishes, and varnishes.* ....We would also like to mention the lead pencils of Messrs Herbin-Fichtenberg and Supersac, which rival the English pencils. The pastel pencils of Mr. Fichtenberg and those of Mr. Pedretti, which are of a suitable hardness to be easily sharpened, do not smear, and are even resistant to being rubbed, must also be mentioned."[7]

"CATALOG OF PRODUCTS OF FRENCH INDUSTRY.
NAMES AND RESIDENCES [OF] MANUFACTURERS AND
ARTISTS ADMITTED TO THE EXHIBITION.
№ 78 FICHTENBERG (Salomon), rue des Bernardins, n. 34:
Fancy paper and pencils. Honorable mention in 1827.
№ 480 FICHTENBERG (Elisabeth; young lady), Paris, rue des Bernadins, n. 34: Embroidery on canvas [needlepoint]."[8]

1835   "FICHTENBERG PENCIL FACTORY IN PARIS. For some time now, shiny varnished pencils in white, black and cedar wood have been on the market, which are distinguished not only by their high quality but also by their high price. In France, however, a large quantity of these pencils also comes from the factory of MR. FICHTENBERG, originally a Prussian manufacturer, who by the way only produces pencils in addition to his marble paper factory. He uses graphite from Briançon [France] and uses clay as a binder. After he has calcined the graphite and mixed it with clay in the appropriate proportion, he has the mixture processed

6   Rapports du jury central, sur les produits de l'industrie française, admis aux expositions Paris. 1832. pp. 163–164.
7   *Archives du Commerce, ou Guide des commerçans, recueil de tous les documens officiels, renseignemens, faits et avis, pouvant intéresser les négocians.* Vol. 5–6 Paris, 1834. p. 79.
8   *Catalogue des produits de l'industrie française...* 1834. p. 32.

in a mill to the greatest degree of consistency and fineness, and then puts it into a metal cylinder and compresses it by means of a screw press in such a way that the mass emerges through the bottom of the cylinder in square or round filaments, depending on the shape of the holes made in the cylinder. As the filament emerges, a worker places it on a flat board, carefully avoiding any bending or stretching of the filament. After drying, the threads are divided into individual sticks. The hardness of the pencil depends on the degree of heating that follows and on the ratio of clay to graphite. Since the pencils nearest the walls of the box are heated more than those in the middle, and thus also become harder, FICHTENBERG has ensured that this disadvantage is avoided by turning the box over more frequently."[9]

1836   *"Colored pencil manufacture*—In France, some hard colored pencils are made by mixing certain metallic oxides with clay. In Germany, the metal oxides and lacquer compounds used to make colored pencils are generally mixed with the smooth, soft-to-the-touch mineral commonly called *soapstone*. M. FICHTENBERG took a different approach; he tried to make colored pencils in much the same way as the grease pencils used in lithography. As the inventor wished to keep his invention secret, we cannot insist on the details. (*Journ. Acad. de l'Indust. June* 1836.)"[10]

1837   "Excerpt from the report of Mr. Merimee on the drawing pencils and colored papers of MR. FICHTENBERG in Paris. From the *Bulletin de la Societe d'encouragement*. August 1836, p, 310.

    "Mr. Fichtenberg, who has already earned great merit for the manufacture of drawing pencils and colored paper in France, has presented the Society with new colored drawing crayons, which, like those intended for lithography, are prepared with a greasy substance, and whose strokes cannot be wiped out by rubbing. These crayons keep the ink very well and can be used for the finest drawings; drawing with them is slower than with the usual pastel crayons, whose shading can be blurred by running the finger over them, but the drawings cannot be erased.

---

9 *Polytechnisches Centralblatt: 1835.* Leipzig. 1835, pp. 255–256.
10 Archives universelles des progrès, inventions, perfectionnemens, découvertes. Paris. 1836.p.411.

"Mr. Fichtenberg is currently producing such crayons from colors, however, they do not form the best chromatic step ladder. The artists will help here, and indicate which colors he should leave out, and which new colors he should make in their place. He knows how to create pencils with each color which possess both the characteristic and the permanence to the same degree.

"Some landscape painters who already used the new crayons assure that this can be done with great advantage and on any kind of white paper. Mr. Fichtenberg believed, however, that he could make the paper even more suitable for this type of drawing by preparing it himself, and for this purpose he covers it with a very white coating which gives it a very fine grain on which the lines turn out more saturated.

"Several artists have prompted Mr. Fichtenberg to concern himself with the manufacture of such pastel colors, which are firmer than those usually used, and which in this respect approximate soft lead pencils. The matter has its great difficulties, for some colors are powdery, and therefore require a binder which binds the molecules into a pulpy and solid paste; others, however, are so solid that they require a binder which reduces their excessive cohesion. Nevertheless, Mr. Fichtenberg is expected to solve this difficult task.

"As for the colored papers...which were coated with a very glossy varnish, and...could be gilded, the varnish of these papers—which for some 20 years made by Zippel in Dresden and for 5 to 6 years by Dessauer in Aschaffenburg—is watery in nature. It is prepared with the so-called *psyllium seed*, i.e., the seed of *Plantago Psyllium*, which was obtained from France. Mr. Fichtenberg knew this well. Only after a great number of laborious attempts did he succeed in finding the technique which is necessary if the fabrications are to succeed perfectly. The new French papers are more economical than the German ones which have a significant import duty; also, the German manufacturers seem to mix the psyllium mucilage with a different gum for the sake of convenience, which makes the papers less supple and somewhat brittle. The coating on the French papers is uniform; even the application of the gold, which otherwise had its difficulties because of the greater thickness of the beaten gold, goes quite well and easily.

"In addition, Mr. Fichtenberg has also invented a new type of marbled paper, which he wants to be used especially for wall-papering dining rooms. The Society therefore awarded him its gold medal in recognition of all these services rendered to French industry." [11]

1839   *"Marbled papers; by M.* FICHTENBERG.

"Marbled, solid-colored papers are manufactured in Germany, and are coated with a very shiny varnish which gives them the property of being gilded without the use of any other primer: this is the aqueous varnish formed by the mucilage extracted from psyllium seed.

"Mr. *Fichtenberg's* papers are made in the same way, but they are softer, and the gilding takes perfectly.

"The marbling they are covered with presents a wide variety of designs, and they combine strength with low cost."[12]

1840   "FICHTENBERG in Paris (rue de la vieille Monnaie, 17,) pencils made of natural graphite cost 2 Fr. a dozen. In relation to their quality (they were too malleable and too and smudging) [they are] too expensive."[13]

1843   [Expired patent notice.] "Chemical and manufacturing improvements in the manufacture of colored papers in imitation of granite and various marbles, and means and processes for lustering, glazing or satinizing them.

"B. of improvement and perfection. [Patent] 10 years old, issued on March 2, 1827, *Fichtenberg and co.*, represented, in Paris, by SOLOMON ASSER-FICHTENBERG of Albert, rue Neuve-Saint-Augustin, № 18."[14]

1844   "M. FICHTENBERG, of Paris, rue de la Vieille-Monnaie, 17, has been manufacturing for a long time a lot of white and colored

11 Dingler, Johann Gottfried. *Dinglers polytechnisches journal*, Volume 63. 1837.
12 *Archives des Decouvertes Et Des Inventions Nouvelles...* Volume 28. Paris. pp. 234–244.
13 Hermann, Friedrich Benedikt Wilhelm. *Die Industrieausstellung zu Paris im Jahre 1839*. Nürnburg, 1840. p. 292.
14 *Description des machines et procedes specifies dans les brevets d'invention, de perfectionnement et d'importation, dont la duree est expirée...* Paris. 1843. p. 203.

items, with relief prints of letters and figures, which are used by several industries.

"The jury gives him an honorable mention."[15]

1844   [On the manufacture of pencils:] "The establishments of Fichtenberg & Co. as well as both Humblot and Conté à Paris have distinguished themselves most in this field of production. In terms of darkness, their products surpass those of English manufacturers, but they lack the fine quality and especially the characteristic luster that gives drawings made with English pencils such a delicate and pleasing appearance."[16]

1849   "M. FICHTENBERG, rue Meslay. 53, reports that after numerous trials he has succeeded in making pure lead pencils, and consequently without mixing clay; he believes that these pencils are equal in quality to those of English manufacture, and even superior by their beautiful velvety black. MR. FICHTENBERG has also devoted himself to making soft pastels according to the procedures of the older generations, the advantages of which he points out: he encloses with his letter samples of pencils, pastels and paper prepared for pastel drawings."[17]

1850   "Mr. *Fichtenberg*, rue Meslay, 53, draws the attention of the Société to Mr. *Jules Sage*, who has held the position of foreman in his establishment for the past seventeen years. Mr. *Fichtenberg* praises Mr. *Sage's* intelligence, activity and integrity, and presents him as a candidate for one of the foremen's medals."[18]

1851   "Mr. *Fichtenberg* has received several awards from the Society; in 1835 and 1839, medals were awarded for his lead pencils and marbled papers.

"Mr. *Fichtenberg* is constantly striving to improve his industry; his new pencils prepared with pure iron carbide and his pastel pencils are pleasant and easy to use for drawing." [19]

---

15 *Eposisition des Produits de L'Industrie Francaise en 1844: Rapport du Jury Central*. Vol. 3. Paris. 1844.p. 623.
16 *Jurende's mährischer Wanderer*. Volume 33. 1844. p. 118.
17 *Société d'encouragement pour l'industrie nationale*. 1849.
18 *Société d'encouragement pour l'industrie nationale*. 1850. p. 625.
19 *Société d'encouragement pour l'industrie nationale*. 1851. p. 253.

"Mr. Sage (Jules). At various times, the Company has been able to admire Mr. *Fichtenberg's* processes for manufacturing marbled papers, iron carbide pencils and pastels. This skilled manufacturer is pleased to recognize Mr. *Jules Sage*, who has held the position of foreman in his establishment for seventeen years, as a useful collaborator, thanks to his zeal and intelligence."[20]

1852   "Formulas for the production of common pastels have scarcely been published, especially since modern chemistry has provided manufacturers with new, beautiful colors, or, through skillful manipulation, has enhanced the tone and nuance of old ones. Those that MR. FICHTENBERG describes in his MANUAL, he guarantees as proven by consummate experience."[21]

1854   SALOMON FICHTENBERG died on April 7, 1855, in Paris.[22]

---

20 *Société d'encouragement pour l'industrie nationale.* 1851. p. 273.
21 *The Technologist: Mitteilungen des Deutsch-Amerikanischen Techniker-Verbandes*, Volume 13. Paris. 1852. p. 279.
22 Archives de Paris, Paris, France. Actes de naissance, de mariage et de décès.

Chromatography; or, a Treatise on Colours and Pigments
By George Field[1]

CHAP. VIII. | WHITE.[2]

I. WHITE WHITE LEAD, or ceruse, and other white oxides of lead, under the various denominations of *London* and *Nottingham whites*, &c. *Flake white*, *Crems* or *Cremnitz white*, *Roman* and *Venetian whites*, *Blanc d'argent* or *Silver white*, *Sulphate of lead*, &c. The heaviest and whitest of these are the best, and in point of colour and body are superior to all other whites. They are all, when pure and properly applied in oil and varnish, safe and durable, and dry well; but excess of oil discolours them, and in water-painting they are changeable even to blackness. They have also a destructive effect upon all vegetal lakes, except the rubial or madder lakes, and madder carmines; they are equally injurious to red and orange leads or *minium*, king's and patent yellow, massicot, gamboge, orpiments, &c.: but ultramarine, red and orange vermilions, yellow and orange chromes, madder colours, Sienna earth, Indian red, and all the ochres, compound with these whites with little or no injury. Cleanliness in using them is necessary for health; for though not virulently poisonous, they are pernicious when taken into or imbibed by the pores or otherwise, as are all other pigments of which lead is the basis.

The following are the true characters of these whites according to our particular experience:

1. LONDON and NOTTINGHAM WHITES. The best of these do not differ in any essential particular mutually, nor from the white leads of other manufactories. The latter, being prepared from flake white, is generally the grayest of the two. The inferior white leads are adulterated with whitening or other earths, which injure them in body and brightness, dispose them to dry more slowly, to keep their place less firmly, and to discolour the oil with which they are applied. All the above are carbonates of lead, and liable to froth or bubble when used with aqueous, spirituous, or acid preparations.

---

1 Field, George. *Chromatography; Or, a Treatise Colours and Pigments And of Their Powers in Painting, &c.,* London. 1835
2 These chapters have been abridged to save space. The original text can be found at https://tinyurl.com/2p8xhdyn.

2. CREMS or CREMNITZ WHITE is a white carbonate of lead, which derives its names from Crems or Krems in Austria, or Kremnitz in Hungaria, and is called also *Vienna* white, being brought from Vienna in cakes of a cubical form. Though highly reputed, it has no superiority over the best English white leads, and varies like them according to the degrees of care or success with which it has been prepared.

3. FLAKE WHITE is an English white lead in form of scales or plates, sometimes gray on the surface. It takes its name from its figure, is equal or sometimes superior to Crems white, and is an oxidised carbonate of lead, not essentially differing from the best of the above.

4. BLANC D'ARGENT, or SILVER WHITE. These are false appellations of a white lead, called also *French white*. It is brought from Paris in the form of drops, is exquisitely white, and has all the properties of the best white leads; but, being liable to the same changes.

5. SULPHATE OF LEAD is an exceedingly white precipitate from any solution of lead by sulphuric acid, much resembling the blanc d'argent; and has, when well prepared, quite neutral, and thoroughly edulcorated or washed, most of the properties of the best white leads, but is sometimes rather inferior in body and permanence.

The above are the principal whites of lead; but there are many other whites used in painting, of which the following are the most worthy of attention:

II. ZINC WHITE is an oxide of zinc, which has been more celebrated as a pigment than used, being perfectly durable in water and oil, but wanting the body and brightness of fine white leads in oil; while in water, constant or barytic white, and pearl white, are superior to it in colour, and equal in durability. Nevertheless, zinc white is valuable, as far as its powers extend in painting, on account of its durability both in oil and water, and its innocence with regard to health.

III. CONSTANT WHITE, PERMANENT WHITE, or *Barytic white*, is a sulphate of barytes, and when well prepared and free from acid, is one of our best whites for water-painting, being of superior body in water, but destitute of this quality in oil.

As it is of a poisonous nature, it must be kept from the mouth;—in other respects and properties it resembles the true pearl white. Both these pigments should be employed with as little gum as possible, as it destroys their body, opacity, or whiteness; and solution of gum ammoniac answers best.

IV. WHITE CHALK is a well-known native carbonate of lime, used by the artist only as a crayon, or for tracing his designs, for which purpose it is sawed into lengths suited to the port-crayon. *White crayons* and *tracing-chalks*, to be good, must work and cut free from grit. From this material *whitening* and lime are prepared, and are the bases of many common pigments and colours used in distemper, paper-staining, &c.

CHAP. IX. | YELLOW.

I. 1. CHROME YELLOW is a pigment of modern introduction into general use, and of considerable variety, which are mostly *chromates of lead*, in which the latter metal more or less abounds. They are distinguished by the pureness, beauty, and brilliancy of their colours, which qualities are great temptations to their use in the hands of the painter; they are notwithstanding far from unexceptionable pigments;—yet they have a good body, and go cordially into tint with white both in water and oil; but, used alone or in tint, they after some time lose their pure colour, and may even become black in impure air; they nevertheless resist the sun's rays during a long time. Upon several colours they produce serious changes, ultimately destroying Prussian and Antwerp blues, when used therewith in the composition of greens, &c.
2. JAUNE MINERALE. This pigment is also a chromate of lead, prepared in Paris, differing in no essential particular from the above, except in the paleness of its colour. The chrome yellows have also obtained other names from places or persons from whence they have been brought, or by whom they have been prepared.

II. PATENT YELLOW. *Turner's Yellow*, or *Montpellier Yellow*, is a submuriate or cloruret of lead, which metal is the basis of most opaque yellow pigments: it is a hard, ponderous, sparkling substance, of a crystalline texture and bright yellow colour; hardly inferior, when ground, to chromic yellow. It has an excellent body, and works well in oil and water, but is soon injured both by the sun's light and impure air; it is therefore little used, except for the common purposes of house-painting, &c.

III. NAPLES YELLOW is a compound of the oxides of lead and antimony, antiently prepared at Naples under the name of *Giallolini;* it is supposed also to have been a native production of Vesuvius and other volcanoes, and is a pigment of deservedly considerable reputation. It is not so vivid a colour as either of the above, but is variously of a pleasing light, warm, yellow tint. Like all the preceding yellows it is opaque, and in this sense is of good body. It is not changed by the light of the sun, and may be used safely in oil or varnish, under the same management as the whites of lead; but, like these latter pigments also, it is liable to change even to blackness by damp and impure air when used as a water-colour, or unprotected by oil or varnish.

Iron is also destructive of the colour of Naples yellow, on which account great care is requisite in grinding and using it not to touch it with the common steel palette-knife, but to compound its tints on the palette with a spatula of ivory or horn. For the same reason it may be liable to change in composition with the ochres, Prussian and Antwerp blues, and all other pigments of which iron is an ingredient or principal; but used purely or with white lead, its affinity with which gives permanency to their tints, it is a valuable and proved colour in oil, in which also it works and dries well.

IV. MASSICOT, or *Masticot,* is an oxide of lead of a pale yellow colour, exceedingly varying in tint from the purest and most tender yellow or straw colour to pale ash colour or gray. It has in painting all the properties of the white lead from which it is prepared, but in tint with which nevertheless it soon loses its colour and returns to white. If, however, it be used pure or unmixed, it is a useful delicate colour, permanent in oil under the same conditions as white lead, but ought not to be employed in water, on account of its changing in colour even to blackness by the action of damp and impure air. It appears to have been prepared with great care, and successfully employed by the old masters.

V. YELLOW OCHRE, called also *Mineral Yellow*, is a native pigment, found in most countries, and abundantly in our own. It varies considerably in constitution and colour, in which latter particular it is found from a bright but not very vivid yellow to a brown yellow, called *spruce ochre,* and is always of a warm cast. Its natural variety is much increased by artificial dressing and compounding. The best yellow ochres are not powerful, but as far as they go are valuable pigments, being neither subject to change by ordinary light, nor much affected by impure air or the action of lime; by time, however, and the direct rays of the sun they are somewhat darkened. Iron is the principal colouring matter in them all, of which the following are the principal species; but they are often confounded:

1. OXFORD OCHRE is a native pigment from the neighbourhood of Oxford, semi-opaque, of a warm yellow colour and soft argillaceous texture, absorbent of water and oil, in both which it may be used with safety according to the general character of yellow ochres, of which it is one of the best. Similar ochres are found in the Isle of Wight, in the neighbourhood of Bordeaux, and various other places.

2. STONE OCHRE has been confounded with the above, which it frequently resembles, as it does also Roman ochre. True stone ochres are found in balls or globular masses of various sizes in the solid body of stones, lying near the surface of rocks among the quarries in Gloucestershire and elsewhere. These balls are of a smooth compact texture, in general free from grit, and of a powdery fracture. They vary exceedingly in colour from yellow to brown, murrey and gray, but do not differ in other respects from the preceding, and may be safely used in oil or water in the several modes of painting, and for browns and dull reds in enamel.

3. DI PALITO is a light yellow ochre, not differing much from the foregoing, but affording tints rather purer in colour than the brightest of them, but less so than Naples yellow. Many pleasing varieties of ochrous colours are produced by burning and compounding with lighter, brighter, and darker colours, but often very injudiciously, and adversely to that simple economy of the palette which is favourable to the certainty of operation, effect, and durability.

4. ROMAN OCHRE is rather deeper and more powerful in colour than the above, but in other respects differs not essentially from them—a remark which applies equally to yellow ochres of other denominations.

5. BROWN OCHRE, *Spruce Ochre*, or *Ochre de Rue*, is a dark-coloured yellow ochre, in no other respect differing from the preceding. It is much employed, and affords useful and permanent tints.

VI. TERRA DI SIENNA, or *Raw-Sienna earth*, &c. is also a ferruginous native pigment, and appears to be an iron ore, which may be considered as a crude natural yellow lake, firm in substance, of a glossy fracture, and very absorbent. It is in many respects a valuable pigment—of rather an impure yellow colour, but has more body and transparency than the ochres; and being little liable to change by the action of either light, time, or impure air, it may be safely used according to its powers, either in oil or water, and in all the modes of practice.

VII. 1. YELLOW ORPIMENT is a sulphurated oxide of arsenic, of a beautiful, bright, and pure yellow colour, not extremely durable in water, and less so in oil—in tint with white lead it is soon destroyed. It is not subject to discolourment in impure air. This property is not, however, sufficient to redeem it with the artist, as it has a bad effect upon several valuable colours; and, although it is not so poisonous as white arsenic, is dangerous in its effect upon health. Yellow orpiment is of several tints, from bright cool yellow to warm orange, the first of which are most subject to change; and it has appeared under various forms and denominations. These seem to have been used by several of the old masters, with especial care to avoid mixture; and as they dry badly, and the oxides of lead used in rendering oils drying destroy their colour.

2. KING'S YELLOW. Yellow orpiment has been much celebrated under this name, as it has also under the denomination of—

3. CHINESE YELLOW, which is a very bright sulphuret of arsenic brought from China.

VIII. 1. PLATINA YELLOW is, as its name implies, a preparation from *platina*, which has afforded the author two fine yellow pigments, the deepest of which resembles the *Terra di Sienna*, but is warmer in tone and richer in colour and transparency, much resembling fine gall-stone. It works well, and is extremely permanent both in water and oil, in which it neither suffers change by the action of the sun, nor of sulphuretted hydrogen and impure air, and is therefore a valuable pigment, and may be produced of many tints. The other is a—
2. LEMON YELLOW, of a beautiful light vivid colour. In body and opacity it is nearly equal to Naples yellow and masticot, but much more pure and lucid in colour and tint, and at the same time not liable to change by damp, sulphureous or impure air, nor by the action of light, nor by the steel palette-knife, nor by mixture with white lead or other pigments, either in water or oil, in each of which vehicles it works welt. Both these pigments are, therefore, valuable additions to the palette.

IX. MADDER YELLOW is a preparation from the madder-root. The best is of a bright colour, resembling *Indian yellow*, but more powerful and transparent, though hardly equal to it in durability of hue—metallic, terrene, and alkaline substances acting on and reddening it as they do gamboge: even alone it has by time a natural tendency to become orange and foxy. We have produced it of various hues and tints, from an opaque and ochrous yellow, to a colour the most brilliant, transparent, and deep. Upon the whole, however, after an experience of many years, we do not consider them eligible pigments.

X. 1. GAMBOGE is brought principally, it is said, from Cambaja in India, and is, we are told, the produce of several trees. The natives of the coast of Coromandel call the tree from which it is principally obtained *Gokathu,* which grows also in Ceylon and Siam. From the wounded leaves and young shoots the gamboge is collected in a liquid state, and dried: indeed our indigenous herb celandine yields, in the same manner, a beautiful yellow juice of the same properties as gamboge. Gamboge is a concrete vegetal substance, of a gum-resinous nature, and beautiful yellow colour, bright and transparent, but not of great depth. Time effects less change in this colour than on other bright vegetal yellows; but white lead and other metallines injure, and terrene and alkaline substances redden it. It works remarkably well in water, with which it forms an opaque solution, without grinding or preparation, by means of its natural gum. In its natural state it however dries well, and lasts in glazing when deprived of its gum. It is perfectly innocent with regard to other colours, and, though it is a strong medicine, is not dangerous or deleterious in use. It has also been employed as a yellow lake prepared upon an aluminous base; but a much better way than either is to dissolve it into a paste in water, and mix it with lemon-yellow, with which pigment being diffused it goes readily into oil or varnish.

2. EXTRACT OF GAMBOGE is the colouring matter of gamboge separated from its greenish gum and impurities by solution in alcohol and precipitation, by which means it acquires a powdery texture, rendering it miscible in oil, &c. and capable of use in glazing. It is at the same time improved in colour, and retains its original property of working well in water with gum.

XI. INDIAN YELLOW, brought from India, as its name implies, is a pigment long employed in India under the name *Pwree*, but has not many years been introduced generally into painting in Europe. It is imported in the form of balls, is of a fetid odour, and is produced from the urine of the camel. It has also been ascribed, in like manner, to the buffalo, or Indian cow, after feeding on mangos; but the latter statement is incorrect. However produced, it appears to be a urio-phosphate of lime, of a beautiful pure yellow colour, and light powdery texture; of greater body and depth than gamboge, but inferior in these respects to gall-stone. Indian yellow resists the sun's rays with singular power in water-painting; yet in ordinary light and air, or even in a book or portfolio, the beauty of its colour is not lasting. It is not injured by foul air, but in oil it is exceedingly fugitive, both alone and in tint. Owing probably to its alkaline nature, it has injurious effect upon cochineal lakes and carmine when used with them.

XII. 1. YELLOW LAKE. There are several pigments of this denomination, varying in colour and appearance according to the colouring substances used and modes of preparation. They are usually in the form of drops, and their colours are in general bright yellow, very transparent, and not liable to change in an impure atmosphere; qualities which would render them very valuable pigments, were they not soon discoloured, and even destroyed, by the opposite influence of oxygen and light, both in water and oil; in which latter vehicle, like other lakes in general, they are bad dryers, and do not stand the action of white lead or metallic colours. If used, therefore, it should be as simple as possible. Of these lakes, the following are the best:

2. QUERCITRON LAKE, or *Quercitron Yellow*, is what its names imply. It is dark in substance, in grains of a glossy fracture, perfectly transparent, and when ground is of a beautiful yellow colour, more durable than the common yellow lakes, although not perfectly permanent.

XIII. DUTCH PINK, ENGLISH and ITALIAN PINKS, are sufficiently absurd names of yellow colours prepared by dyeing, whitening, &c. with vegetal yellow tinctures, in the manner of rose pink, from which they borrow their name.

They are bright yellow colours, extensively used in distemper and for paper-staining, and other ordinary purposes; but are little deserving attention in the higher walks of art, being in every respect inferior even to the yellow lakes, except the best kind of Italian pink, which is, in fact, a yellow lake, and richer in colour than the pigments generally called *yellow lake.*

The pigment called *Stil,* or *Stil de grain,* is a similar preparation, and a very fugitive yellow, the darker kind of which is called *brown-pink.*

CHAP. X. | OF RED.

I. VERMILION is a sulphuret of mercury, which, previous to its being levigated, is called *cinnabar.* It is an ancient pigment and is both found in a native state and produced artificially. Vermilion probably obtained its name from resemblance, or admixture with the beautiful though fugitive colours obtained from the *vermes,* or insects, which yield carmines. The Chinese possess a native cinnabar so pure as to require grinding only to become very perfect vermilion, not at all differing from that imported in large quantities from China: it is said also to be found in abundance in Corinthia, in the Palatinate, Friuli, Bohemia, Almaden in Spain, the principality of Deux-Ponts, and also in South America, particularly in Peru, &c.

Chinese vermilion is of a cooler or more crimson tone than that generally manufactured from factitious cinnabar in England, Holland, and different parts of Europe. The artificial, which was antiently called *minium,* a term now confined to red lead, does not differ from the natural in any quality essential to its value as a pigment; it varies in tint from dark red to scarlet; and both sorts are perfectly durable and unexceptionable pigments—the most so perhaps of any we possess, when pure. It is true, nevertheless, that vermilions have obtained the double disrepute of fading in a strong light and of becoming black or dark by time and impure air: but colours, like characters, suffer contamination and disrepute from bad association; it has happened accordingly that vermilion which has been rendered lakey or crimson by mixture with lake or carmine, has faded in the light, and that when it has been toned to the scarlet hue by red or orange lead it has afterwards become blackened in impure air, &c. both of which adulterations were formerly practised, and hence the ill fame of vermilion both with authors and artists. We therefore repeat, that neither light, time, nor foul air, effect sensible change in true vermilions, and that they may be used safely in either water, oil, or fresco—being colours of great chemical permanence, unaffected by other pigments, and among the least soluble of chemical substances.

Good vermilion is a powerful vivid colour of great body, weight, and opacity;—when pure it will be entirely decomposed and dissipated by fire in a red heat, and is therefore, in respect to the above mixtures, easily tested.

II. RED LEAD, *Minium,* or *Saturnine Red,* by some old writers confounded with cinnabar, and called *Simper* or *Synoper,* is an oxide of lead of a scarlet colour and fine hue, warmer than common vermilion; bright, but not so vivid as the iodide of mercury, though it has the body and opacity of both these pigments, and has been confounded, even in name, with vermilion, with which it was formerly customary to mix it. When pure and alone, light does not affect its colour; but white lead, or any oxide or preparation of that metal mixed with it, soon deprives it of colour, as acids do also; and impure air will blacken and ultimately metallize it.

On account of its extreme fugitiveness when mixed with white lead, it cannot be used in tints; but employed, unmixed with other pigments, in simple varnish or oil not rendered drying by any metallic oxide, it may, under favourable circumstances, stand a long time; hence red lead has had a variable character for durability. As regards colour, it cannot be mixed safely with any other pigments than the ochres, earths, and blacks in general: when employed in water the reds of lead, iodine, and mercury are warmed and brightened in colour by the addition of gum; this it does mechanically by allowing the darker particles to subside.

III. RED OCHRE is a name proper rather to a class, than to an individual pigment, and comprehends *Indian red, light red, Venetian red, scarlet ochre, Indian ochre, redding, ruddle, bole,* &c. beside other absurd appellations, such as *English vermilion* and *Spanish brown,* or *majolica.*

Almagra, the *Sil Atticum* of the ancients, is a deep red ochre found in Andalusia, as is also their *terra Sinopica, See.* or *Armenian bole,* dug originally in Cappadocia, and now found in New Jersey and elsewhere under the name of *bloodstone.*

The red ochres are, for the most part, rather hues and tints than definite colours, or more properly classed with the tertiary, semi-neutral, and broken colours; they are, nevertheless, often very valuable pigments for their tints in dead colouring, and for their permanence, &c. in water, oil, crayons, and fresco. The greater part of them are native pigments, found in most countries, and very abundantly and fine in our own; but some are productions of manufacture, and we have produced them in the variety of nature by art. The following are the most important of these pigments, most of which are available in enamel-painting.

1. INDIAN RED, according to its name, is brought from Bengal, and is a very rich iron ore, or per-oxide of iron. It is an anomalous red, of a purple-russet hue, of a good body, and valued when fine for the pureness and lakey tone of its tints. In a crude state it is a coarse powder, full of extremely bard and brilliant particles of a dark appearance, sometimes magnetic, and is greatly improved by grinding and washing over. Its chemical tendency is to deepen, nevertheless it is very permanent; neither light, impure air, mixture with other pigments, time, nor fire, effecting in general any sensible change in it; but, being opaque, and not keeping its place well, it is of course not fit for glazing. This pigment varies considerably in its hues—that which is most rosy being esteemed the best, and affording the purest tints: inferior red ochres have been formerly substituted for it, and procured it a variable character, but it is now obtained abundantly, and may be had pure of respectable colourmen.

Persian Red is another name for this pigment, for which we have often heard the late Presidents, Mr. West, Sir Thomas Lawrence, and others, well experienced in its use, express the highest esteem.

2. LIGHT RED is an ochre of a russet-orange hue, principally valued for its tints. The common light red is brown ochre burnt, but the principal yellow ochres afford this colour best; and the brighter and better the yellow ochre is from which this pigment is prepared, the brighter will this red be, and the better flesh tints will it afford with white. There are, however, native ochres brought from India and other countries which supply its place, some of which are darkened by time and impure air; but in other respects light red has the general good properties of other ochres, dries admirably, and is much used both in figure and landscape. It affords also an excellent crayon.

3. TERRA PUZOLLI is a species of light red, as is also the *carnagione* of the Italians, which differs from the above only in its hue, in which respect other variations and denominations are produced by dressing and compounding.

4. VENETIAN RED, or *Scarlet Ochre.* True Venetian red is said to be a native ochre, but the colours sold under this name are prepared artificially from sulphate of iron, or its residuum in the manufacturing of acids. They are all of redder and deeper hues than light red, are very permanent, and have all the properties of good ochres.

Prussian red and *English red* are other names for the same pigment.

5. SPANISH RED is an ochre differing little from Venetian red.

IV. DRAGON'S BLOOD is a resinous substance, brought principally from the East Indies. It is of a warm semi-transparent, rather dull, red colour, which is deepened by impure air, and darkened by light. There are two or three sorts, but that in drops is the best. *White lead* soon destroys it, and it dries with extreme difficulty in oil. It is sometimes used to colour varnishes and lackers; but, notwithstanding it has been recommended as a pigment, it does not merit the attention of the artist.

V. LAKE, a name derived from the *lac* or *lacca* of India, is the cognomen of a variety of transparent red and other coloured pigments of great beauty, prepared for the most part by precipitating coloured tinctures of dyeing drugs upon alumine and other earths, &c. The lakes are hence a numerous class of pigments, both with respect to the variety of their appellations and the substances from which they are prepared. The colouring matter of common lake is brazilwood, which affords a very fugitive colour. Superior red lakes are prepared from cochineal, lac, and kermes; but the best of all ere those prepared from the root of the *rubia tinctoria,* or madder plant. Of the various red lakes the following are the principal:

1. RUBRIC, or MADDER LAKES. These pigments are of various colours, of which we shall speak at present of the red or rose colours only; which have obtained, from their material, their hues, or their inventor, the various names of rose rubiates, rose madder, pink madder, and Field's lakes.

The pigments formerly called *madder lakes* were brick-reds of dull ochrous hues; but for many years past these lakes have been prepared perfectly transparent, and literally as beautiful and pure in colour as the rose; qualities in which they are unrivalled by the lakes and carmine of cochineal. The rose colours of madder have justly been considered as supplying a desideratum, and as the most valuable acquisition of the palette in modern times, since perfectly permanent transparent reds and rose-colours were previously unknown to the art of painting.

2. LIQUID RUBIATE, or *Liquid Madder Lake,* is a concentrated tincture of madder of the most beautiful and perfect rose colour and transparency. It is used as a water-colour only in its simple state diluted with pure water, without gum; nevertheless, as it were by a sort of seeming caprice, it dries quicker in oil than alone or in water, by acting as a dryer to the oil. Mixed or ground with all other madder colours without gum, they form combinations which work freely in simple water, and produce the most beautiful and permanent effects. Liquid rubiate affords also a fine red ink—and is a durable stain which bears washing, for marking, painting, or printing on cotton or linen cloth, &c.

3. SCARLET LAKE is prepared in form of drops from cochineal, and is of a beautiful transparent red colour, and excellent body, working well both in water and oil, though, like other lakes, it dries slowly. Strong light discolours and destroys it both in water and oil; and its tints with white lead, and its combinations with other pigments, are not permanent; yet when well prepared and judiciously used in sufficient body, and kept from strong light, it has been known to last many years; but it ought never to be employed in glazing, nor at all in performances that aim at high reputation and durability. It is commonly tinted with vermilion, which has probably been mixed with lakes at all times to give them scarlet hue and add to their weight; for upon examining with a powerful lens some fine pictures of ancient masters, in which lake had been used in glazing, particles of vermilion were apparent, from which lake had evidently flown: unfortunately, however, these lakes are injured by vermilion as they are by lead, so that glazings of cochineal lake over vermilion or lead are particularly apt to vanish. This effect is very remarkable in several pictures of Cuyp, in which he has introduced a figure in red from which the shadows have disappeared, owing to their having been formed with lake over vermilion.

4.   HAMBURGH LAKE is a lake of great power and depth of colour, purplish, or inclining to crimson, which dries with extreme difficulty, but differs in no other essential quality from other cochineal lakes—an observation which applies to various lakes under the names of *Roman Lake, Venetian Lake,* and many others; not one of which, however respectively beautiful or reputed, is entitled to the character of durability either in hue, shade, or tint.

5.   KERMES LAKE is the name of an ancient pigment, perhaps the earliest of the European lakes; which name is sometimes spelt *cermes,* whence probably *cermosin* and *crimson,* and *kermine* or *carmine.* In some old books it is called *vermilion,* in allusion to the insect, or *vermes,* from which it is prepared; a title usurped probably by the sulphuret of mercury or cinnabar, which now bears the name of vermilion. This lake is prepared from the kermes, which formerly supplied the place of cochineal. We have obtained the kermes from Poland, where it is still collected; and some with which we have been favoured was brought from Cefalonia by Colonel C. J. Napier, who states that it is employed by the modern Greeks for dying their caps red. This substance and the lac of India probably afforded the lakes of the Venetian painters, and of the earliest painters in oil of the school of Van Eyck. Some old specimens of the pigment which we obtained were in drops of a powdery texture and crimson colour, warmer than cochineal lakes, and having less body and brilliancy, but worked well, and withstood the power of light better than the latter, though the sun ultimately discoloured and destroyed them. In all other respects they resemble the lakes of cochineal.

6.   LAC LAKE is prepared from the lac or lacca of India, and is perhaps the first of the family of lakes. Its colouring matter resembles those of the cochineal and kermes, in being the production of a species of insects. Its colour is rich, transparent, and deep—less brilliant and

more durable than those of cochineal and kermes, but inferior in both these respects to the colours of madder. Used in body or strong glazing, as a shadow colour, it is of great power and much permanence; but in thin glazing it changes and flies, as it does also in tint with white lead.

A great variety of lakes, equally beautiful as those of cochineal, have been prepared from this substance in a recent state in India and China, many of which we have tried, and found uniformly less durable in proportion as they were more beautiful. In the properties of drying, &c. they resemble other lakes.

This appears to have been the lake which has stood best in old pictures, and was probably used by the Venetians, who had the trade of India when painting flourished at Venice. It is sometimes called *Indian Lake*.

7.   CARMINE, a name originally given only to the fine feculences of the tinctures of kermes and cochineal, denotes generally at present any pigment which resembles them in beauty, richness of colour, and fineness of texture: hence we hear of blue and other coloured carmines, though the term is principally confined to the crimson and scarlet colours produced from cochineal by the agency of tin. These carmines are the brightest and most beautiful colours prepared from cochineal—of a fine powdery texture and velvety richness. They vary from a rose colour to a warm red; work admirably; and are in other respects, except the most essential—the want of durability, excellent pigments in water and oil. They have not, however, any permanence in tint with white lead, and in glazing are soon discoloured and destroyed by the action of light, but are little affected by impure air, and are in other respects like the lakes of cochineal; all the pigments prepared from which may be tested by their solubility in liquid ammonia, which purples lakes prepared from the woods, but does not dissolve their colours.

8.   MADDER CARMINE, or *Field's Carmine*, is, as its name expresses, prepared from madder. It differs from the rose lakes of madder principally in texture, and in the greater richness, depth, and transparency of its colour, which is of various hues from rose colour to crimson. These in other respects resemble the rubric or madder lakes, and are the only *durable carmines* for painting either in water or oil; for both which their texture qualifies them without previous grinding or preparation.

9.   ROSE PINK is a coarse kind of lake, produced by dying chalk or whitening with decoction of brazilwood, &c. It is a pigment much used by paper-stainers, and in the commonest distemper painting, &c., but is too perishable to merit the attention of the artist.

CHAP. XI. | OF BLUE.

I. ULTRAMARINE, *Lazuline, Azurine,* or *Azure,* is prepared from the lapis lazuli, a precious stone found principally in Persia and Siberia. It is the most celebrated of all modern pigments, and, from its name and attributes, is probably the same as the no less celebrated *Armenian blue,* or *Cyanus,* of the ancients. Of the latter, Theophrastus informs us that the honour of inventing its factitious preparation (by perhaps the very singular chemico-mechanical process still in use for ultramarine) was ascribed in the Egyptian annals to one of their kings; and it was so highly prized that the Phoenicians paid their tribute in it, and it was given in presents to princes: hence it was a common practice in those times to counterfeit it. Our opinion of the identity of these pigments is considerably strengthened by the accounts modern travellers give of the brilliant blue painting still remaining in the ruins of temples in Upper Egypt, which is described as having all the appearance of ultramarine. Add to this, also, that the Chinese have the art of preparing this pigment; and as they are imitators, and rarely inventors, and cannot be supposed to have learnt it of the Europeans, it is to be inferred that they possess it as an ancient art: that they have it, we conclude from having received specimens of this pigment, of a good colour, direct from Canton. In China, too, the lapis lazuli is highly esteemed, and is worn by mandarines as badges of nobility conferred only by the emperor; which remarkably coincides with the ancient usage related by Theophrastus.

Ultramarine has not obtained its reputation upon slight pretensions, being, when skilfully prepared, of the most exquisitely beautiful blue, varying from the utmost depth of shadow to the highest brilliancy of light and colour—transparent in all its shades, and pure in its tints. It is of a true medial blue, when perfect, partaking neither of purple on the one hand, nor of green on the other: it is neither subject to injury by damp and impure air, nor by the intensest action of light, and it is so eminently permanent that it remains perfectly unchanged in the oldest paintings; and there can be little doubt that it is the same pigment which still continues with all its original force and beauty in the temples of Upper Egypt, after an exposure of at least three thousand years. The ancient Egyptians had, however, other blues, of which we have already mentioned their counterfeit Armenian blue; and we have lately seen some balls of blue pigment, of considerable depth and purity of colour, in the collection of Mr. Sams, obtained by him from the ruins of Upper Egypt, which is probably of the same kind. The Egyptians had also several vitreous blues, with which they decorated their figures and mummies.

The immense price of ultramarine in former times was almost a prohibition to its use; but the spirit of modern commerce having supplied its material more abundantly, and the discoveries and improvement of Prussian, Antwerp, and cobalt blues, having furnished substitutes for its ordinary uses, it may now be obtained at moderate prices, particularly its lighter and very useful tints.

Pure ultramarine varies in shade from light to dark, and in hue from pale warm azure to the deepest cold blue; the former of which, when impure in colour, is called *ultramarine ashes*.

II. FACTITIOUS ULTRAMARINE, *French Ultramarine, Outremere de Guimet, Bleu de Garance*, &c. In some of the latter numbers of "Brande's Journal," are accounts of a process for producing *factitious* ultramarine; and a variety of these have been before the public under the above and other names. These pigments are in general of deep rich blue colours, darker and less azure than fine ultramarine of the same depths, and answering to the same acid tests, but variously affected by fire and other agents: none of them, however, possess the merits of genuine ultramarine, and their relative value to other blues remains to be determined by mature experience. An experiment in which this blue was tried by an ingenious artist and friend of the author, however, speaks little in its favour. He took a picture, the sky of which had been recently painted in the ordinary manner with *Prussian blue* and white; and having painted on the clear part of the sky uniform portions with tints formed of the best *factitious ultramarine, cobalt blue*, and *genuine ultramarine*, so as to match the ground of the sky, and to disappear to the eye thereon by blending with the ground, when viewed at a moderate distance, he set the picture aside for some months; after which it appeared upon examination that the colour of these various blue pigments had taken different ways, and departed from the hue of the ground. The factitious ultramarine had *blackened*—the cobalt blue *greened*—the *true ultramarine* appeared of a *pure azure*, like a spot of light—and their ground, the Prussian blue sky, appeared by contrast with the ultramarine of a *gray* or *slate colour*.

III. 1. COBALT BLUE is the name now appropriated to the modern improved blue prepared with metallic cobalt, or its oxides, although it properly belongs to a class of pigments including *Saxon blue, Dutch ultramarine, Royal blue, Hungary blue, Smalt, Zaffre* or *Enamel blue*, and *Dumont's blue*. These differ principally in their degrees of purity, and the nature of the earths with which they are compounded.

The first is the finest cobalt blue, and may not improperly be called a *blue lake*, the colour of which is brought up by fire, in the manner of enamel blues; and it is, when well prepared, of a pure blue colour, neither tending to green nor purple, and approaching in brilliancy to the finest ultramarine. It has not however the body, transparency, and depth, nor the natural and modest hue, of the latter; yet it is superior in beauty to all other blue pigments. Cobalt blue works better in water than ultramarine in general does, and is hence an acquisition to those who have not the management of the latter, and also on account of its cheapness. It resists the action of strong light and acids; but its beauty declines by time, and impure air greens and ultimately blackens it.

Various appellations have been given to this pigment from its preparers and venders, and it has been called *Vienna blue, Paris blue, azure,* and, very improperly, *ultramarine.*

IV.   1.   PRUSSIAN BLUE, otherwise called *Berlin blue, Parisian blue, Cyanide of Iron,* &c., is rather a modern pigment, produced by the combination of the prussic or hydro-cyanic acid and iron. It is of a deep and powerful blue colour, of vast body and considerable transparency, and forms tints of much beauty with white lead, though they are by no means equal in purity and brilliancy to those of cobalt and ultramarine, nor have they the perfect durability of the latter.

Prussian blue lasts a long time under favourable circumstances, its tints fade by the action of strong light, and it is purpled or darkened by damp or impure air. It becomes greenish also sometimes by a development of the yellow oxide of iron. The colour of this pigment has also the singular property of fluctuating or of going and coming under some changes of circumstances, and time has a neutralizing tendency upon its colour.

2.   ANTWERP BLUE is a lighter-coloured and somewhat brighter Prussian blue, or ferro-prussiate of alumine, having more of the terrene basis, but all the other qualities of that pigment, except its extreme depth. *Haerlem Blue* is a similar pigment.

V.   1.   INDIGO, or *Indian Blue,* is a pigment manufactured in the East and West Indies from several plants, but principally from the anil or indigofera. It is of various qualities, and has been long known, and of great use in dyeing. In painting it is not so bright as Prussian blue, but is extremely powerful and transparent; hence it may be substituted for some of the uses of Prussian blue. It is of great body, and glazes and works well both in water and oil. Its relative permanence as a dye has obtained it a false character of extreme durability in painting, a quality in which it is nevertheless very inferior even to Prussian blue.

It is injured by impure air, and in glazing some specimens are firmer than others, but not durable;—in tint with white lead they are all fugitive; when used, however, in considerable body in shadow, it is more permanent, but in all respects inferior to Prussian blue.

2.   INTENSE BLUE is indigo refined by solution and precipitation, in

which state it is equal in colour to Antwerp blue. By this process indigo also becomes more durable, and much more powerful, transparent, and deep. It washes and works admirably in water;—in other respects it has the common properties of indigo. We have been assured by an eminent architect, equally able and experienced in the use of colours, that these blues of indigo have the property of pushing or detaching Indian ink from paper. The same is supposed to belong to other blues; but as this effect is chemical, it can hardly be an attribute of mere colour.

VI. 1. BLUE VERDITER is a blue oxide of copper, or precipitate of the nitrate of copper by lime, and is of a beautiful light blue colour. It is little affected by light; but time, damp, and impure air turn it green, and ultimately blacken it—changes which ensue even more rapidly in oil than in water: it is therefore by no means an eligible pigment in oil, and is principally confined to distemper painting and the uses of the paper-stainer, though it has been found to stand well many years in water-colour drawings and in crayon paintings, when preserved dry.
2. SAUNDERS BLUE, a corrupt name, from *Cendres Bleus*, the original denomination probably of *ultramarine ashes,* is of two kinds, the natural and the artificial: the artificial is a verditer prepared by an alkali from sulphate of copper; the natural is a blue mineral found near copper-mines, and is the same as—
3. MOUNTAIN BLUE, found in similar situations as the above. A very beautiful substance of this kind, a *carbonate of copper*, both blue and green, is found in Cumberland. None of these blues of copper are, however, durable: used in oil, they become green, and as pigments are precisely of the character of verditers.
4. SCHWEINFURT BLUE appears to be the same in substance as Scheele's green, prepared without heat or treated with an alkali. It is a beautiful colour, liable to the same changes, and is of the same habits as blue verditer and the above pigments.

VII. BLUE BICE, *Iris* or *Terre Bleu*, is sometimes confounded with the above copper blues; but the true bice is said to be prepared from the *lapis Armenius* of Germany and the Tyrol, and is a light bright blue. The true Armenian stone of the ancients was probably the lapis lazuli of later times, and the blue prepared therefrom the same as our ultramarine.

VIII. BLUE OCHRE is a mineral colour of rare occurrence, found in Cornwall, and also in North America, and is a *sub-phosphate of iron.* What Indian red is to the colour red, and Oxford ochre to yellow, this pigment is to the colour blue; they class in likeness of character;—hence it is admirable rather for the modesty and solidity than for the brilliancy of its colour. It has the body of other ochres, more transparency, and is of considerable depth. It works well both in water and oil, dries readily, and does not suffer in tint with white lead, nor change when exposed to the action of strong light, damp or impure air: it is therefore, as far as its powers extend, an eligible pigment, though it is not in general use, nor easily procurable. It answers to the same acid tests as ultramarine, and is distinguishable from it by changing from a blue phosphate to an olive-brown ochrous oxide of iron when exposed to a red heat. It has been improperly called *native Prussian blue.*

IX. BLUE CARMINE is a blue oxide of molybdena, of which little is known as a substance or as a pigment. It is said to be of a beautiful blue colour, and durable in a strong light, but is subject to be changed in hue by other substances, and blackened by foul air: we may conjecture, therefore, that it is not of much value in painting.

CHAP. XII. | OF ORANGE.

I. MIXED ORANGE. Orange being a colour compounded of red and yellow, the place of original orange pigments may be supplied by mixture of the two latter colours; by glazing one over the other; by stippling, or other modes of breaking and intermixing them in working, according to the nature of the work and the effect required. For reasons before given, mixed pigments are inferior to the simple or homogeneous in colour, working, and other properties: yet some pigments mix and combine more cordially and with better results than others; this is the case with the *liquid rubiate* and *gamboge,* and they form the best and most durable mixed orange of all hues for painting in water. In oil the compounding of colours is more easily effected.

II. ORANGE VERMILION is a sulphuret of quicksilver or vermilion of an orange colour, newly introduced: it resembles red lead in appearance, but is not subject to its changes, being a perfectly durable pigment under every circumstance of oil or water painting. Its tints are much warmer than those of red or orange lead; and it is a most powerful tinger of white, yielding purer and more delicate warm carnation tints than any known pigment, and much resembling those of Titian and Rubens. It is the best and only unexceptionable orange we possess, drying in simple linseed oil, and having the powerful body and properties of the other vermilions, and may be tested in the same manner. It works with best effect in water with a considerable portion of gum.

III.   1.   CHROME ORANGE is a beautiful orange pigment, and is one of the most durable and least exceptionable chromates of lead, and not of iron, as it is commonly called, being truly a subchromate of lead.

It is, when well prepared, of a brighter colour than red, or orange vermilion, but is inferior in durability and body to the latter pigment, being liable to the changes and affinities of the chrome yellows in a somewhat less degree, but less liable to change than the orange oxide of lead (v.) following.

2.   LAQUE MINERAL is a French pigment, a species of chromic orange, similar to the above. This name is also given to orange oxide of iron.

3.   CHROMATE OF MERCURY is improperly classed as a red with vermilion, for though it is of a bright ochrous red colour in powder, it is, when ground, of a bright orange ochre colour, and affords with white very pure orange-coloured tints. Nevertheless it is a bad pigment, since light soon changes it to a deep russet colour, and foul air reduces it to extreme blackness.

IV.   1.   ORANGE OCHRE, called also *Spanish ochre,* &c. is a very bright yellow ochre burnt, by which operation it acquires warmth, colour, transparency, and depth. In colour it is moderately bright, dries and works well both in water and oil, and is a very durable and eligible pigment. It may be used in enamel-painting, and has all the properties of its original ochre in other respects.

2.   JAUNE DE MARS is an artificial iron ochre, similar to the above, of which we formerly prepared a variety brighter, richer, and more transparent than the above.

3.   DAMONICO, or *Monicon,* is also an iron ochre, being a compound of Terra di Sienna and Roman ochre burnt, and having all their qualities. It is rather more russet in hue than the above, has considerable transparency, is rich and durable in colour, and affords good flesh tints.

4.   BURNT SIENNA EARTH is, as its name expresses, the *Terra di Sienna* burnt, and is of an orange russet colour. What has been said of orange ochre and Damonico may be repeated of burnt Sienna. It is richer in colour, deeper, and more transparent, and works better than *raw Sienna earth;* but, in other respects, has all the properties of its parent colour, and is permanent and eligible wherever it may be useful.

5.   LIGHT RED and VENETIAN RED, before treated of, are also to be considered as impure, but durable, orange colours; and several artificial preparations of iron afford excellent colours of this class.

V.   ORANGE LEAD is an oxide of lead of a more vivid and warmer colour than *red lead,* but, in other respects, does not differ essentially from that pigment.

VI. ORANGE ORPIMENT, or *Realgar,* improperly called also *Red Orpiment,* since it is of a brilliant orange colour, inclining to yellow. There are two kinds of this pigment; the one, *native,* the other, *factitious;* the first of which is called *sandarach,* &c., and is of rather a redder colour than the factitious. They are the same in qualities as pigments, and differ not otherwise than in colour from *yellow orpiment,* to which the old painters gave the orange hue by heat, and then called it *alchymy.*

VII. MADDER ORANGE, *ox Orange Lake,* is a madder lake of an orange hue, varying from yellow to rose-colour and brown. This variety of madder colours differs not essentially in other respects from those of which we have already spoken, except in a tendency toward redness in the course of time.

CHAP. XIII. | OF GREEN.

I. MIXED GREENS. Green being a compound of *blue* and *yellow,* pigments of these colours may be used to supply the place of green pigments, by compounding them in the several ways of working—by mixing, glazing, hatching, or otherwise blending them in the proportions of the various hues required. The fine nature-like greens, which have lasted so well in some of the pictures of the Italian schools, appear to have been compounded of ultramarine and yellow. Whatever pigments are employed on a picture in the warm yellow hues of the foreground, and blue colouring of the distance and sky, are advantageous for forming the greens in landscape, &c., because they harmonize better both in colouring and chemically, and impart homogeneity to the whole—which is a principle conducive to a fine tone and durability of effect; and this is a principle which applies to all mixed colours. In compounding colours, it is desirable not only that they should agree chemically, but that they should also have, as much as may be, the same degree of durability; and in these respects Prussian or Antwerp blue and gamboge form a judicious, though not extremely durable, compound, similar to *Varley's green, Hooker's green,* &c.

There is a green pigment of this kind prepared in Rome, of which the late President of the Royal Academy brought home a quantity, the modern substitute probably of the *Italian green* above mentioned, but wanting its durability, as it becomes blue in fading, and appears to be a mixture of Prussian blue and Dutch or Italian pink.

II. TERRE-VERTE. True Terre-Verte is an ochre of a bluish green colour not very bright, in substance moderately hard, and smooth in texture. It is variously a bluish or gray coaly clay combined with yellow oxide of iron or yellow ochre. Although not a bright, it is a very durable pigment, being unaffected by strong light and impure air, and combining with other colours without injury. It has not much body, is semitransparent, and dries well in oil. There are varieties of this pigment; but the green earths which have copper for their colouring matter are, although generally of brighter colours, inferior in their other qualities, and are not true terre-vertes.

The greens called *Verona green*, and *Verdetto*, *or holy green*, are similar native pigments of a warmer colour. These greens are found in the Mendip Hills, France, Italy, and the Island of Cyprus.

III.   CHROME GREENS, commonly so called, are compound pigments, of which chrome yellow is the principal colouring substance. These are also called *Brunswick green*, &c. and are compounds of chromate of lead with Prussian and other blue colours, constituting fine greens to the eye, suitable to some of the ordinary purposes of mechanic art; but for obvious reasons before given are unfit for fine art. There is, however, a true chrome green, or *Native green*, the colouring matter of which is the pure oxide of chrome, and, being free from lead, is durable both against the action of the sun's light and impure air. It is of various degrees of transparency or opacity, and of several hues more or less warm or cool, which are all rather fine than brilliant greens, and afford pure and durable tints. True Chrome greens neither give nor receive injury from other pigments, and are eligible for either water or oil painting, in the latter of which they dry rapidly.

IV.   COBALT GREENS. There are two pigments of this denomination, the one a compound of cobalt blue and chromic yellow, which partakes of the qualities of those pigments, and may be formed on the palette—the other, an original pigment prepared immediately from cobalt, which is of a pure but not very powerful green colour, and durable both in water and oil, in the latter of which it dries well.

V.   1.   COPPER GREEN is the appellation of a class rather than of an individual pigment, under which are comprehended *Verdigris, Verditer, Malachite Mineral green, Green bice, Scheele's green*, *Schweinfurt* or *Vienna green,* Emerald green, *true* Brunswick green, green Lake, Mountain green, African green, French green, Saxon green, Persian green, Patent green. Marine green, Olympian great, *&c.;* and old authors mention others under the names of individuals who prepared them, such are *Verde de Barildo,* &c.

The general characteristics of these greens are, brightness of colour, well suited to the purposes of house-painting, but not adapted to the modesty of nature in fine art. They have considerable permanence, except from the action of damp and impure air, which ultimately blacken them, to which shade they have also a tendency by time. They have a good body, and dry well in oil, but, like the whites of lead, are all deleterious substances. We will particularize the principal sorts:

2. VERDIGRIS, or *Viride AEris*, is of two kinds, common or impure, and crystallized or *Distilled Verdigris*, or more properly refined verdigris. They are both acetates of copper, of a bright green colour inclining to blue. They are the least permanent of the copper greens, soon fading as water-colours by the action of light, &c. and becoming first white and ultimately black by damp and foul air. In oil verdigris is durable with respect to light and air, but moist and impure air change its colour, and cause it to effloresce or rise to the surface through the oil. It dries rapidly, and might be useful as a siccific with other greens or very dark colours. In varnish it stands better, but is not upon the whole a safe or eligible pigment, either alone or compounded. Vinegar dissolves it, and the solution is used for tinting maps, &c.

3. GREEN VERDITER is the same in substance as blue verditer, which is converted into green verditer by boiling. This pigment has the common properties of the copper greens above mentioned, and is sometimes called *Green Bice*.

4. EMERALD GREEN is the name of a new copper green upon a terrene base. It is the most vivid of this tribe of colours, being rather opaque and powerfully reflective of light, and appears to be the most durable pigment of its class. Its hue is not common in nature, but well suited for gems or glazing upon. It works well in water, but difficultly in oil, and dries badly therein.

5. MINERAL GREEN is the commercial name of *green lakes*, prepared from the sulphate of copper. These vary in hue and shade, have all the properties before ascribed to copper greens, and afford the best common greens, and, not being liable to change of colour by oxygen and light, stand the weather well, and are excellent for the use of the house-painter, &c.; but are less eligible in the nicer works of fine art, having a tendency to darken by time and foul air.

6. MOUNTAIN GREEN is a native carbonate of copper, combined with a white earth, and often striated with veins of mountain blue, to which it bears the same relation that green verditer does to blue verditer, nor does it differ from these and other copper greens in any property essential to the painter. The *Malachite*, a beautiful copper ore, employed by jewellers, is sometimes called *mountain green*, and *Green bice* is also confounded therewith, being similar substances and of similar use as pigments.

VI. SCHEELE'S GREEN is a compound oxide of copper and arsenic, named after the justly celebrated chemist who discovered it. It is variously of a beautiful light warm green colour, opaque, permanent in itself and in tint with white lead, but must be used cautiously with Naples yellow, by which it is soon destroyed. *Schweinfurt green* is the name of a fine preparation of the same kind. Both these pigments are less affected by damp and impure air than the simple copper greens, and are therefore in these respects rather more eligible colours than copper greens in general.

VII. PRUSSIAN GREEN. The pigment celebrated under this name is an imperfect prussiate of iron, or Prussian blue, in which the yellow oxide of iron superabounds, or to which yellow tincture of French berries has been added, and is not in any respect superior as a pigment to the compounds of Prussian blue and yellow ochre.

VIII. SAP GREEN, or *Verde Vessie,* is a vegetal pigment prepared from the juice of the berries of the buckthorn, the green leaves of the woad, &c. It is usually preserved in bladders, and is thence sometimes called *Bladder Green;* when good it is of a dark colour and glossy fracture, extremely transparent, and of a fine natural green colour. Though much employed as a water-colour without gum, which it contains naturally, it is a very imperfect pigment, disposed to attract the moisture of the atmosphere, and to mildew; and, having little durability in water-colour painting, and less in oil, it is not eligible in the one, and is totally useless in the other.

Similar pigments, prepared from coffee-berries, and called *Venetian* and *emerald greens,* are of a colder colour, very fugitive, and equally defective as pigments.

CHAP. XIV. | OF PURPLE.

I. MIXED PURPLES. Purple being a secondary colour, composed of *blue and red*, it follows of course that any blue and red pigments, which are not chemically at variance, may be used in producing mixed purple pigments of any required hue, either by compounding or grinding them together ready for use, or by combining them in the various modes of operation in painting. In such compounding, the more perfect the original colours are, the better in general will be the purple produced. In these ways *ultramarine* and the *rose colours of madder* constitute excellent and beautiful purples, which are equally permanent in water

and oil, in glazing, or in tint, whether under the influence of the oxyge-
nous or the hydrogenous principles of light and impure air, by which
colours are subject to change. The blue and red of cobalt and madder
afford also good purples. Some of the finest and most delicate purples
in ancient paintings appear to have been similarly compounded of *ultramarine* and *vermilion*, which constitute tints equally permanent, but
less transparent than the above. Facility of use, and other advantages,
are obtained at too great a sacrifice by the employment of perishable
mixtures, such as are the carmines and lakes of cochineal with *indigo*
and other *blue colours*.

II.   MADDER PURPLE, *Purple Rubiate*, or *Field's Purple*, is a very
rich and deep carmine, prepared from madder. Though not a brilliant
purple, its richness, durability, transparency, and superiority of colour, have given it the preference to the purple of gold preceding, and
to burnt carmine. It is a pigment of great body and intensity; it works
well, dries and glazes well in oil, and is pure and permanent in its tints.
It neither gives nor sustains injury from other colours, and is in every
respect a very perfect and eligible pigment.

There is a lighter and brighter sort, which has all the properties of
the above with less intensity of colour.

III.   BURNT CARMINE is, according to its name, the carmine of cochineal partially charred till it resembles in colour the purple of gold, for
the uses of which in miniature and water-painting it is substituted,
and has the same properties except its durability; of which quality,
like the carmine it is made from, it is deficient, and therefore in this
important respect is an ineligible pigment. A durable colour of this
kind may, however, be obtained by burning *madder carmine* in a cup
over a spirit lamp, or otherwise, stirring it till it becomes of the hue
or hues required.

IV.   PURPLE LAKE. The best purple lake is prepared from cochineal,
and is of a rich and powerful colour, inclined to crimson. Its character
as a pigment is that of the cochineal lakes already described. It is fugitive both in glazing and tint; but, used in considerable body, as in the
shadows of draperies, &c. it will last under favourable circumstances
a long time. Lac lake resembles it in colour, and may supply its place
more durably, although not perfectly so.

V.   PURPLE OCHRE, or MINERAL PURPLE, is a dark ochre, native
of the Forest of Dean in Gloucestershire. It is of a murrey or chocolate
colour, and forms cool tints of a purple hue with white. It is of a similar

body and darker colour than *Indian red*, which has also been classed among purples, but in all other respects it resembles that pigment.

CHAP. XV. | OF CITRINE.

I. MIXED CITRINE. What has been before remarked of the mixed secondary colours is more particularly applicable to the tertiary, it being more difficult to select three homogeneous substances, of equal powers as pigments, than two, that may unite and work together cordially. Hence the mixed tertiaries are still less perfect and pure than the secondaries; and as their hues are of extensive use in painting, original pigments of these colours are proportionately estimable to the artist. Nevertheless there are two evident principles of combination, of which the artist may avail himself in producing these colours in the various ways of working; the one being that of combining two original secondaries—e. g. *green and orange* in producing a *citrine;* the other, the uniting the three primaries in such a manner that *yellow* predominate in the case of citrine, and *blue and red* be subordinate in the compound.

These colours are, however, in many cases produced with best and most permanent effect, not by the intimate combination of pigments upon the palette, but by intermingling them, in the manner of nature, on the canvas, so as to produce the effect at a proper distance of a uniform colour. Such is the *citrine* colour of fruit and foliage; on inspecting the individuals of which we distinctly trace the stipplings of orange and green, or yellow, red, and green. Similar beautiful consonances are observable in the *russet* hues of foliage in the autumn, in which purple and orange have broken or superseded the uniform green of leaves; and also in the *olive* foliage of the rose-tree, produced in the individual leaf by the ramification of purple in green. Yet mixed citrines may be compounded safely and simply by slight additions, to an original brown pigment, of that primary or secondary colour which is requisite to give it the required hue.

II. BROWN PINK is a vegetal lake precipitated from the decoction of French berries, and dyeing woods, and is sometimes the residuum of the dyer's vat. It is of a fine rich transparent colour, rarely of a true brown; but being in general of an orange broken by green, it falls into the class of citrine colours, sometimes inclining to greenness, and sometimes toward the warmth of orange. It works well both in water and oil, in the latter of which it is of great depth and transparency, but dries badly.

Its tints with white lead are Very fugitive, and in thin glazing it does not stand. Upon the whole, it is more beautiful than eligible.

III. CITRINE LAKE is a more durable and better drying species of brown pink, prepared from the quercitron bark.

IV. UMBER, commonly called *Raw Umber,* is a natural ochre, abounding with oxide of manganese, said to have been first obtained from ancient Ombria, now Spoleto, in Italy;—it is found also in England, and in most parts of the world; but that which is brought from Cyprus, under the name of Turkish umber, is the best. It is of a brown-citrine colour, semi-opaque, has all the properties of a good ochre, is perfectly durable both in water and oil, and one of the best drying colours we possess. Although not so much employed as formerly, it is perfectly eligible according to its colour and uses.

Several browns, and other ochrous earths, approach also to the character of citrines; such are the terre de Cassel, &c. But in the mixed confusion of names, infinity of tones and tints, and variations of individual pigments, it is impossible to attain an unexceptionable or universally satisfactory arrangement;—we have therefore followed a middle and general course in distributing pigments under their proper heads.

CHAP. XVI. | OF RUSSET.

I. MIXED RUSSET. What has been remarked in the preceding chapter upon the production of mixed citrine colours, is equally applicable in general to the mixed russets: we need not therefore repeat it. By the immediate method of producing it materially from its secondaries, orange vermilion and madder purple afford a compound russet pigment of a good and durable colour. Chrome orange and purple lake yield a similar but less permanent mixture.

Many other less eligible duple and triple compounds of russet are obvious upon principle, and it may be produced by adding red in due predominance to some browns; but all these are inferior to the following original pigments:

II. RUSSET RUBIATE, *Madder Brown,* or *Field's Russet,* is, as its names indicate, prepared from the *rubia tinctoria,* or madder-root. It is of a pure, rich, transparent, and deep russet; of a true middle hue between orange and purple; not subject to change by the action of light, impure air, time, nor mixture of other pigments. It has supplied a great desideratum, and is indispensable in water-colour painting, both as a local and auxiliary colour, in compounding and producing with yellow the glowing hues of autumnal foliage, &c., and with blue the beautiful and endless variety of grays in skies, flesh, &c. There are three kinds of this pigment, distinguished by variety of hue, russet, or *madder brown*, *orange russet*, and purple russet, or *intense madder brown*; which differ not essentially in their qualities as pigments, but as warm or cool russets, and are all good glazing colours. The last dries best in oil, the others but indifferently.

III.   PRUSSIATE OF COPPER differs chemically from Prussian blue only in having copper instead of iron for its basis. It varies in colour from russet to brown, is transparent and deep, but, being very liable to change in colour by the action of light and by other pigments, has been very little employed by the artist.

There are several other pigments which enter imperfectly into, or verge upon, the class of russet, which, having obtained the names of other classes to which they are allied, will be found under other heads; such are some of the ochres and Indian red. Burnt carmine and Cassius's precipitate are often of the russet hue, or convertible to it by due additions of yellow or orange; as burnt Sienna earth and various browns are, by like additions of lake or other reds.

CHAP. XVII. | OF OLIVE.

I.   MIXED OLIVE may be compounded in several ways; directly, by uniting *green* and *purple,* or by adding to *blue* a smaller proportion of *yellow* and *red,* or by breaking much blue with little orange. Cool black pigments, combined with yellow ochre, afford eligible olives. These hues are called *green* in landscape, and *invisible green* in mechanic painting. It is to be noted that, in producing these and other compound colours on the palette or canvas, those mixtures will most conduce to the harmony of the performance which are formed of pigments otherwise generally employed in the picture.

II.   BURNT VERDIGRIS is what its name expresses, and is an olive-coloured oxide of copper deprived of acid. It dries remarkably well in oil, and is more durable; and, in other respects, an improved and more eligible pigment than the original verdigris. Scheele's green affords by burning also a series of similar olive colours, which are as durable as their original pigment.

III. OLIVE LAKE is a lake prepared from the green ebony, and is of considerable durability, transparency, and great depth, both in water and oil, in which latter vehicle it dries well.

CHAP. XVIII. | OF BROWN.

I. VANDYKE-BROWN. This pigment, hardly less celebrated than the great painter whose name it bears, is a species of peat or bog-earth of a fine, deep, semi-transparent brown colour. The pigment so much esteemed and used by Vandyke is said to have been brought from Cassel; and this seems to be justified by a comparison of *Cassel-earth* with the browns of his pictures. The Vandyke-browns in use at present appear to be terrene pigments of a similar kind, purified by grinding and washing over: they vary sometimes in hue and in degrees of drying in oil, which they in general do tardily, owing to their bituminous nature, but are good browns of powerful body, and are durable both in water and oil. The *Campania-brown* of the old Italian painters was a similar earth.

II. MANGANESE BROWN is an oxide of manganese, of a fine, deep, semi-opaque brown of good body, which dries admirably well in oil. It is deficient of transparency, but may be a useful colour for glazing or lowering the tone of white without tinging it, and as a local colour in draperies, dead-colouring, &c. It is a perfectly durable colour both in water and oil.

III. CASSEL-EARTH, or, corruptly, *Castle-earth.* The true *terre de Cassel* is an ochrous pigment similar to the preceding, but of a brown colour, more inclined to the russet hue. In other respects it does not differ essentially from Rubens' and Vandyke-browns.

IV. COLOGN-EARTH, incorrectly called *Cullen's-earth,* is a native pigment, darker than the two last, and in no respect differing from Vandyke-brown in its uses and properties as a colour. Similar earths abound in our own country.

V. BURNT UMBRE is the fossil pigment called *Umbre,* burnt, by which it becomes of a deeper and more russet hue, and very drying in oil, in which it is employed as a dryer. It may be substituted for Vandyke-brown, and is a perfectly durable and eligible pigment in water, oil, or fresco. The old Italians called it *falsalo.*

VI. BONE BROWN and *Ivory Brown* are produced by torrefying, or roasting, bone and ivory till by partially charring they become of a brown colour throughout. They may be made to resemble the five first browns above by management in the burning; and, though much esteemed by some artists, are not perfectly eligible pigments, being bad dryers in oil, and their lighter shades not durable either in oil or water when exposed to the action of strong light, or mixed in tint with white lead. The palest of these colours are also the most opaque: the deepest are more durable, and most so when approaching black.

VII. MUMMY, or *Egyptian Brown,* is also a bituminous substance combined with animal remains, brought from the catacombs of Egypt, where liquid bitumen was employed three thousand years ago in embalming, in which office it has combined, by a slow chemical change, during so many ages with substances which give it a more solid and lasting texture than simple asphaltum; but in this respect it varies exceedingly, even in the same subject. Its other properties and uses as a pigment are the same as those of asphaltum, for which it is employed as a valuable substitute.

VIII. BISTRE is a brown pigment extracted by watery solution from the soot of wood-fires, whence it retains a strong pyroligneous scent. It is of a wax-like texture, and of a citrine-brown colour, perfectly durable. It has been much used as a water-colour, particularly by the old masters in tinting drawings and shading sketches, previously to Indian ink coming into general use for such purposes. In oil it dries with the greatest difficulty.

A substance of this kind collects at the back of fire-places in cottages where peat is the constant fuel burnt; which, purified by solution and evaporation, affords a fine bistre. Scotch bistre is of this kind. All kinds of bistre attract moisture from the atmosphere.

IX. SEPIA, *Seppia, or Animal AEthiops.* This pigment is named after the sepia, or *cuttle-fish,* which is called also the *ink-fish* from its affording a dark liquid which was used as an ink by the ancients. From this liquid our pigment sepia, which is brought principally from the Adriatic, and may be obtained from the fish on our own coasts, is said to be obtained; and it is supposed that it enters into the composition of the *Indian ink* of the Chinese. Sepia is of a powerful dusky brown colour, of a fine texture, works admirably in water, combines cordially with other pigments, and is very permanent.

X. HYPOCASTANUM, or *Chestnut Brown*, is a *brown lake* prepared from the horse-chestnut; transparent and rich in colour, warmer than brown pink, and very durable both in water and oil; in the latter of which it dries moderately well.

XI. PRUSSIAN BROWN is a preparation of Prussian blue, from which the blue colouring principle has been expelled by fire, or extracted by an alkaline ley; it is an orange brown, of the nature and properties of Sienna earth.

CHAP. XIX | OF MARRONE.

I. MARRONE LAKE is a preparation of madder of great depth, transparency, and durability of colour. It works well in water, glazes and dries in oil, and is in all respects a good pigment: as, however, its hues are easily given with other pigments, it has not been much used. There is a deeper kind, which has been called *purple-black.*

II. CARUCRU, or *Chica,* is a new pigment, of a soft powdery texture, and rich marrone colour, brought by Lieutenant Mawe from South America; for a portion of which we have been indebted to the kindness of Mr. Brockedon. It is said to be procured from a species of begonia in the manner of indigo. Comparatively as a pigment, it resembles marrone lake in colour, and is equal in body and transparency to the carmine of cochineal, though by no means approaching it in beauty, or even in durability, fugitive as the latter pigment is. Exposed to the light of a window, even without sun, the colour of carucru is soon changed and destroyed, which defects alone render it unfit for fine art, whatever value it may be found to possess in dyeing or in medicine.

CHAP. XX. | OF GRAY.

I. MIXED GRAYS are formed not only by the compounding of black and white, which yields *neutral greys*, and of black and blue, black and purple, black and olive, &c., which yield the *semi-neutral grays* of clouds, &c., but these may be well imitated by the mixture of russet rubiate, or madder browns, with blues, which form transparent compounds, which are much employed: Grays are, however, as above remarked, so easily produced, that the artist will in this respect vary and suit his practice to his purpose.

II. ULTRAMARINE ASHES are the recrement of Lapis lazuli, from which ultramarine has been extracted, varying in colour from dull gray to blue. Although not equal in beauty, and inferior in strength of colour, to ultramarine, they are extremely useful pigments, affording grays much more pure and tender than such as are composed of black and white, or other blues, and better suited to the pearly tints of flesh, foliage, the grays of skies, the shadows of draperies, &c., in which the old masters were wont to employ them. Ultramarine broken with black and white, &c., produces the same effects, and is thus sometimes carried throughout the colouring of a picture.

III. PHOSPHATE OF IRON is a native ochre, which classes in colour with the deeper hues of ultramarine ashes, and is eligible for all their uses. It has already been described under its appellation of *blue ochre.*

Slate clays and several native earths class with grays; but the colours of some of the latter, which we have tried, are not durable, being subject to become brown by the oxidation of the iron they contain.

CHAP. XXI. | OF THE NEUTRAL, BLACK.

I. IVORY BLACK and Bone *Black* are ivory and bone charred to blackness by strong heat in closed vessels. These pigments vary principally through want of care or skill in preparing them: when well made, they are fine neutral blacks, perfectly durable and eligible both for oil and water painting; but when insufficiently burnt they are brown, and dry badly; and when too much burnt, they are cineritious, opaque, and faint in colour. Of the two, ivory affords the best pigment; but bone black is commonly used, and immense quantities are consumed with sulphuric acid in manufacturing of *shoe-blacking.*

II. LAMP-BLACK, or *Lamblack,* is a smoke black, being the soot of resinous woods, obtained in the manufacturing of tar and turpentine. It is a pure carbonaceous substance of a fine texture, intensely black, and perfectly durable, but dries badly in oil. This pigment may be prepared extemporaneously for water painting by holding a plate over the flame of a lamp or candle, and adding gum-water to the colour: the nearer the plate is held to the wick of the lamp, the more abundant and warm will be the hue of the black obtained; at a greater distance it will be more effectually charred and blacker.

III. FRANKFORT BLACK is said to be made of the lees of wine from which the tartar has been washed, by burning, in the manner of ivory black. Similar blacks are prepared of *vine twigs and tendrils,* which contain tartar; also from *peach-stones,* &c. whence *Almond black;* and the Indians employ for the same purpose the *shell of the cocoa-nut;* and inferior Frankfort black is merely the levigated charcoal of woods, of which the hardest, such as the *box* and *ebony,* afford the best. Fine Frankfort black, though almost confined to copper-plate printing, is one of the best black pigments we possess, being of a fine neutral colour, next in intensity to lamp black, and more powerful than that of ivory. Strong light has the effect of deepening its colour; yet the blacks employed in the printing of engravings have proved of very variable durability.

IV. BLUE BLACK is also a well-burnt and levigated charcoal, of a cool neutral colour, and not differing in other respects from the common Frankfort black above mentioned. Blue black was formerly much employed in painting, and, in common with all carbonaceous blacks, has, when duly mixed with white, a preserving influence upon that colour in two respects, which it owes, chemically, to the bleaching power of carbon, and, chromatically, to the neutralizing and contrasting power of black with white.

V. SPANISH BLACK is a soft black, prepared by burning *cork* in the manner of Frankfort and ivory blacks; and it differs not essentially from the former, except in being of a lighter and softer texture. It is subject to the variation of the above charred blacks.

VI. MINERAL BLACK is a native impure oxide of carbon, of a soft texture, found in Devonshire. It is blacker than plumbago, and free from its metallic lustre—is of a neutral colour, greyer and more opaque than ivory black—forms pure neutral tints—and being perfectly durable, and drying well in oil, it is valuable in dead colouring on account of its solid body, as a preparation for black and deep colours before glazing. It would also be the most durable and best possible black for frescos.

VII. BLACK OCHRE is a variety of the above, combined with iron and alluvial clay. It is found in most countries, and should be washed and exposed to the atmosphere before it is used. Sea-coal, and innumerable black mineral substances have been and may be employed as succedanea for the more perfect blacks, when the latter are not procurable.

Potash

The term potash can be used to refer to a number of different things and can lead to confusion. The material that follows is taken from *Potash Salts: Their Uses and Occurrence in the United States* by W. C. Phalen[1]. This booklet was printed by the Government Printing Office in 1911. It went into great detail about the production, importation, and chemistry of potash. Only the information relevant to the making of fancy paper has been included here.

POTASH.

Under the head of potash are included *potassium carbonate* and *caustic potash*. Potassium carbonate is made from *potassium chloride* by the LeBlanc process, in the same way as soda ash from salt, but the ammonia process can not be employed, because the acid carbonate of potassium ($KHCO_3$) is soluble in ammoniacal solutions and does not precipitate. The material is sold in the trade under the name *potash* or *pearlash* and is used chiefly in the glass industry, in the manufacture of caustic potash, and in the manufacture of *chromates of potassium*. A considerable quantity is bought by soap makers and causticized, the solution being used for soft soaps.

Caustic potash (KOH) is made in the same way as *caustic soda*. It is much more deliquescent than the corresponding sodium compound and is generally made where it is to be used. In soap making it was formerly customary to saponify the fat with caustic potash and then to add common salt. An interchange between the potassium and sodium took place, the result being a hard sodium soap. But as soda is now cheaper than potash and yields a hard soap directly, potash soaps are used only for special purposes.

ALUMS.

In the manufacture of *potash alum* ($K_2SO_4Al_2(SO_4)_3.24H_2O$), large quantities of potassium sulphate are used. On the addition of the potassium sulphate to the sulphate of alumina, the potash alum crystallizes out

---

1   The original document is available at https://books.google.com/books/about/ Potash_salts.html?id=l3BBAQAAMAAJ

in extremely pure form. Alum is extensively used in the dyeing industry as a mordant and by paper makers and leather dressers. A small
quantity is used in medicine.

CYANIDES AND DERIVED COMPOUNDS.

The class of cyanides comprises *potassium cyanide*, or *white prussiate of potash*; sodium cyanide and other simple cyanides, including
cyan-salt, a mixture of potassium and sodium cyanides; *potassium
ferrocyanide* (yellow prussiate of potash); *potassium ferricyanide* (red
prussiate of potash).

Potassium ferrocyanide ($K_4Fe(CN)_6.3H_2O$), also called *yellow prussiate of potash*, is made by fusing together potassium carbonate, iron
borings, and nitrogenous organic matter of any kind, such as horn, hair,
blood, wool waste, and leather scraps. The material in its pure form is
produced in splendid large lemon-yellow crystals. It is not poisonous.
It is largely used for making Prussian blue; in calico printing and in
dyeing; for case-hardening iron; for making *potassium cyanide* and *ferricyanide*; and to a small extent in explosives and as a chemical reagent.

Potassium ferricyanide, or *red prussiate of potash* (K_3FeCN_6), is
usually made by passing chlorine gas into a solution of the ferrocyanide
until ferric chloride no longer forms a precipitate, but produces only
a brown color in the liquid. It may also be made by exposing the dry
powdered ferrocyanide to chlorine until a test portion dissolved in water
gives nothing but a brown color, with ferric chloride. With ferrous
salts, it gives the blue pigment *Turnbull's blue*. Its solution with caustic potash is a powerful oxidizing liquid and as such is used in calico
printing for a "discharge" on indigo and other dyes. It also forms part
of the sensitive coating of blueprint papers.

DYESTUFFS.

Potash salts enter into the dyeing industry chiefly in the form of *alum*.
Potassium sulphide is frequently used to improve the "fire" in vermilion. *Potassium bichromate* is extensively used in the manufacture of
chrome green.

GENERAL CHEMICALS.

Under the heading of general chemicals potash enters into the composition of a host of substances. Some of these are *arsenite of potassium*,
used in the dyeing industry; *bromide of potassium*, used in photography
and medicine; *chlorate of potassium*, used in fireworks, matches, and
aniline colors; *chromate of potassium*, used, in dyeing and electric-

ity; *manganate* and *permanganate of potassium*, used in dyeing and bleaching, in disinfectants, and in medicine; *silicate of potassium*, used in making ordinary yellow soaps, as a fixative for pigments in calico printing, as a vehicle for pigments in fresco painting, for rendering cloth and paper noninflammable, etc.; *cream of tartar*; and argols[2].

ORGANIC SOURCES OF POTASH SALT.

The organic sources of potash salts are wood ashes, beet-sugar molasses and residues, wool scourings (suint), and sea weed.

WOOD ASHES.

Land plants take up considerable quantities of potassium compounds from the soil. When the plants are burned, about 10 per cent of the weight of the ash is *potassium carbonate*, which may be obtained by lixiviation. Potash from wood ashes is now made chiefly in Russia, Sweden, and America, the woods most employed being elm, maple, and birch. Sometimes the stumps and small branches only are burned, the trunks being used for timber. The ashes are moistened slightly, put into tanks having false bottoms on which straw is spread, and then lixiviated with warm water. The *lye* so obtained is evaporated (sometimes by the waste heat from the burning wood) in iron pots until it solidifies on cooling. The dirty brown mass is then calcined in a reverberatory furnace until all the organic matter is destroyed. The product is known as *potash* or *crude pearlash*. It is white or gray in color, and contains about 70 per cent of K_2CO_3, with some *potassium sulphate*, *potassium chloride*, and sodium salts. By redissolving the crude potash in water and settling and concentrating the solution until the sulphates and chlorides separate as crystals, a concentrated and fairly pure lye is obtained. When this is evaporated to dryness and the residue calcined, it yields a much purer product, known as *refined pearlash*, containing from 95 to 97 per cent of K_2CO_3. It is necessary that low heat be employed in the calcination, for the charge fuses at a moderate temperature.

Quicklime is often put in the bottom of the tanks before the ashes are introduced. On leaching, the solution of potassium salts reacts with the lime, forming insoluble calcium salts and yielding more or less potassium hydroxide in the lye. The resulting product is a mixture of potash and caustic potash.

2   *argol—Potassium tartrate* or *dipotassium tartrate*

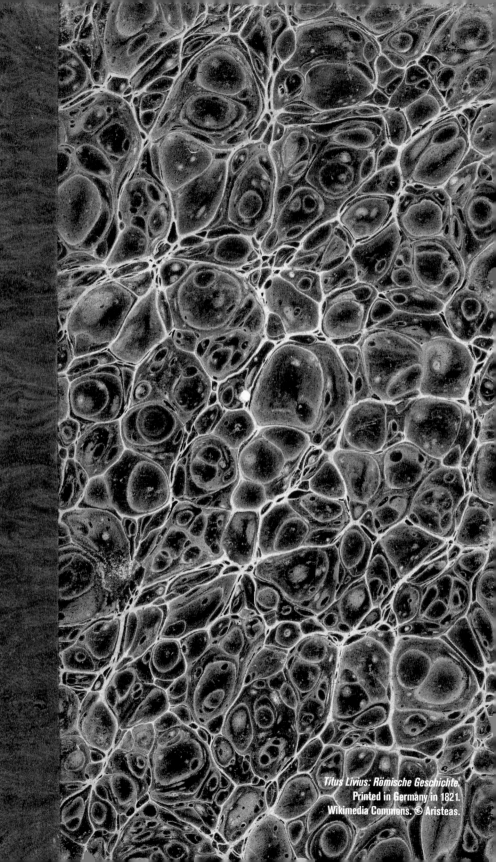

Examples

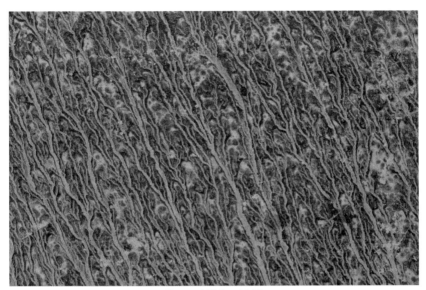

Rome. 1636 or 1647
Wikimedia Commons. ⓒ ⓝ Mr.Nostalgic.

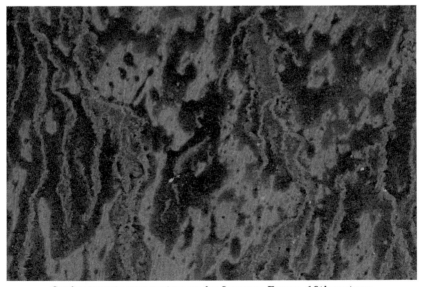

Confessionario muy copioso en dos Lenguas. France, 19th century.
The British Museum.

Diuerse imprese accommodate a diuerse moralità, 1549.
Published in Lione Per Masseo Buonhomo.
Wikimedia Commons. ⊛ Fæ.

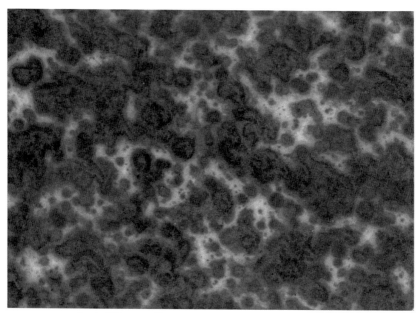

Louis XI., tragedie en cinq actes et en vers. Paris, 1832.
The British Museum.

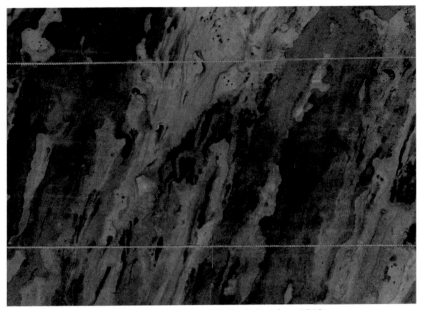

Wallace; or, the Fight of Falkirk. London, 1810.
The British Library.

Aphorismi. Sprinkled calfskin. Paris, 1811.
The British Library.

EXAMPLES

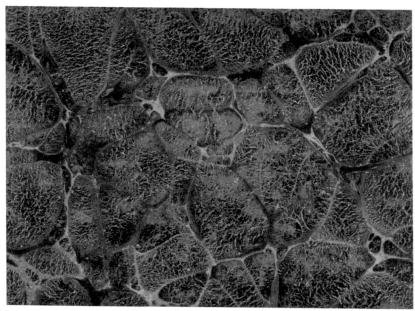

Biblia sacra vulgatæ editionis, etc. 19th century. French binding.
The British Library.

Cahier D'Arabesques. France. Unknown date.
Cooper Hewitt, Smithsonian Design Museum.

SUPPLEMENTAL MATERIAL

Napoleon. Paris, 1840.
The British Library.

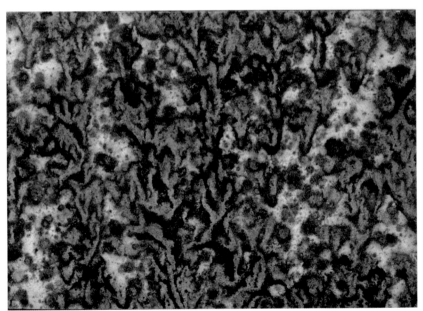

Chefs-d'oeuvre dramatiques. Paris, 1824.
© The British Library.

EXAMPLES

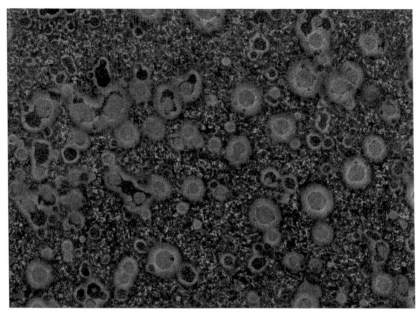

Les Derniers adieux de la Mare. Sprinkled calfskin. Barcelona, 1823.
The British Library.

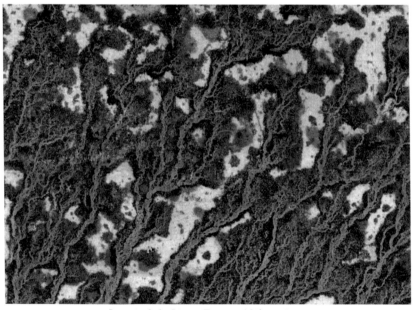

Lesprit de la Ligue. France, 19th century.
The British Library.

SUPPLEMENTAL MATERIAL

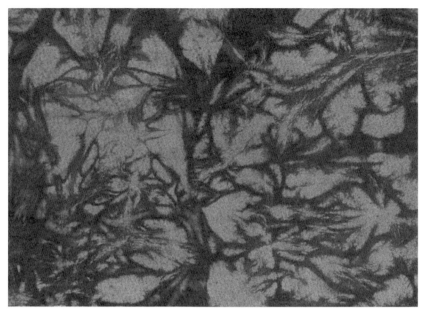

Historia de la conquista de Mexico, etc. Sheepskin. Spain, 18th century.
The British Library.

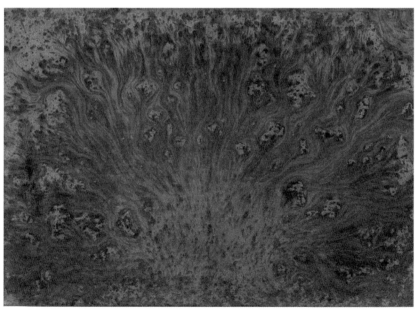

*Private Memoirs relative to the last Year of the Reign of Lewis the
Sixteenth, late King of France.* Calfskin. England, 18th century.
The British Library.

EXAMPLES   225

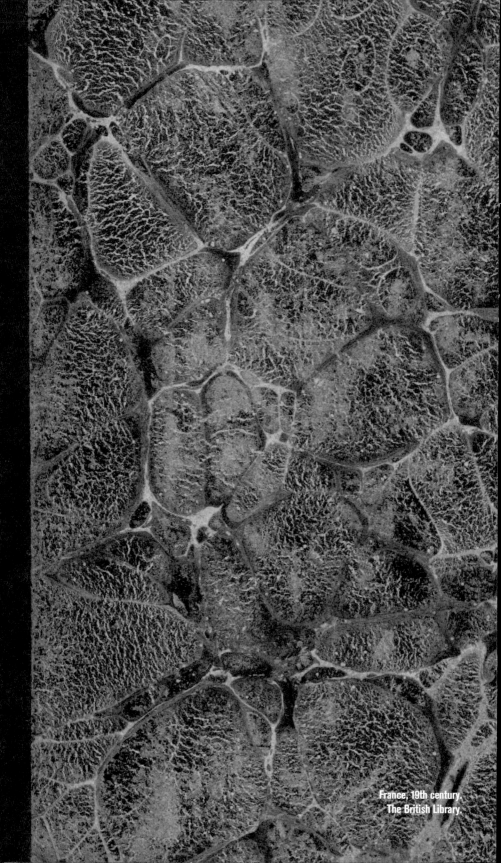

Resources

Online Collections of Decorative Paper

The **University of Washington's University Library** has an extensive online collection of decorative paper samples. It contains scanned samples of both marbled paper and many of the more unusual papers described in this book.
https://content.lib.washington.edu/dpweb/index.html

The Met's **Thomas J. Watson Library** has an online collection called the Paper Legacy Project Collection. It features marbled and paste papers and also includes scans of the *Ink & Gall* newsletter.
https://cdm16028.contentdm.oclc.org/digital/collection/p16028coll21/search

Also Available from Six Penny Graphics

The Progress of the Marbling Art from
Technical Scientific Principles with a
Supplement on the Decoration of Book Edges

By Josef Halfer

140 pages | 6 × 9 | Full color.
ISBN: 978-1732659506

The Whole Art of Marbling as
applied to Paper, Book Edges, Etc

By C. W. Woonough

138 pages | 6 × 9 | Full color.
ISBN: 978-1732659513

Marbled Paper & Whatnot: An Eclectic Collection
of Texts and Assorted Clippings

Includes the *1811 Oswestry* text, *The Mysterious Marbler* by James
Sumner, the above titles by Halfer and Woolnough, and more.

Compiled by Debra G. Tremper

520 pages | 6 × 11 | Full color.
ISBN: 978-1732659551

The Marbling Art: Instructions for Comb
and Turkish Marble for Bookbinders

By J. A. F. Schade
Translated by Debra G. Tremper

42 pages | 5 × 8 | Full color.
ISBN: 978-1732659537

Formulas for Bookbinders

By Louis H. Kinder

134 pages | 6 × 9
ISBN: 978-1732659520

Made in the USA
Las Vegas, NV
24 November 2023

81422942R00148